D1445824

Work *and* Leis
in the Middle Ea

WISSER MEMORIAL LIBRARY

Work *and* Leisure *in the* Middle East

The Common Ground of Two Separate Worlds

Robert A. Stebbins

Transaction Publishers

New Brunswick (U.S.A.) and London (U.K.)

mbibu

WISSER MEMORIAL LIBRARY

HD4904.6
.S73
2013
Copy1

Copyright © 2013 by Transaction Publishers, New Brunswick, New Jersey.

All rights reserved under International and Pan-American Copyright Conventions. No part of this book may be reproduced or transmitted in any form or by any means, electronic or mechanical, including photocopy, recording, or any information storage and retrieval system, without prior permission in writing from the publisher. All inquiries should be addressed to Transaction Publishers, Rutgers—The State University of New Jersey, 35 Berrue Circle, Piscataway, New Jersey 08854-8042. www.transactionpub.com

This book is printed on acid-free paper that meets the American National Standard for Permanence of Paper for Printed Library Materials.

Library of Congress Catalog Number: 2012009390
ISBN: 978-1-4128-4947-0
Printed in the United States of America

Library of Congress Cataloging-in-Publication Data

Stebbins, Robert A., 1938-
Work and leisure in the Middle East : the common ground of two separate
  worlds / Robert A. Stebbins.
     p. cm.
  Includes bibliographical references and index.
     1. Leisure--Middle East. 2. Leisure--Africa, North. 3. Work. 4. Community development--Middle East. 5. Community development--Africa, North. I. Title.
HD4904.6.S73 2012
306.3'60956--dc23

                                                        2012009390

To Irving Louis Horowitz

Contents

Illustrations

Preface

Although the Muse for this book had been in me for several years, it took a reading of Hichem Djaït's excellent *Islamic Culture in Crisis* to finally set me on the road to writing it. Then, as I began to put pen to paper, parts of the Arab/Iranian Middle East and North Africa (MENA) began to erupt in one of the region's biggest social upheavals ever. Dubbed the "Arab Spring" by the Western press, a main grievance of its prime movers—youth, many of whom are unemployed—was and continues to be the acute lack of a democratic say in their countries' governance and an equally objectionable lack of opportunity to develop themselves as individuals. For them this volatile combination of bleak conditions conjures up a dark future.

Leisure and community involvement are rarely directly mentioned in the mass media's coverage and analysis of these stirring events and changes in the MENA. Yet, leisure and community involvement (a special form of leisure) have always formed a significant part of life in the region, and they show every sign of becoming even more significant in the future. This book, the first of its kind, shows why this is true. It also examines how such leisure can be pursued to the benefit of the individual and his or her community.

In fact, the MENA is a region tightly gripped by a developmental crisis. The crisis about which I am writing is a cultural one, however; it centers on how Arabs and Iranians can, through leisure, work, and community involvement, find self-fulfillment, and how they can realize their own potential as human beings and members of their local communities. Interesting material could be written about, for example, economic development or resource development, but those topics would require another book and fall beyond my professional expertise.

The present book, especially in chapters 5 through 8, might be seen as the West giving advice to the people of the MENA. In many countries around the world, such "meddling," such paternalism, is often unwelcome, with the Arab/Iranian Middle East being no exception. At the same time, new ideas for solving a local problem do sometimes come from outside the group or society whose problem it is, with those ideas then being adapted to the culture of the people.

Sometimes they reach this solution without external help, and sometimes they do so aided by outsiders. This is the spirit of this book: it offers leisure and community involvement as ways to personal and social development that people in the MENA may adapt to their lives and societies. This book, then, is better thought of as a dissertation on collective self-help rather than a prescriptive manual, where self-help takes advantage of relevant knowledge whatever its origin.

Arabs in the MENA, Hichem Djaït (2011) declares at various points in his recent book, must embrace modernity as it has evolved in Europe over the past five hundred years or so. This includes embracing democracy, liberty, the value of ordinary life for the ordinary person, the rights of men and women, and respect for others and thereby for self, the community, and civil society. These are some of the key values of modernity. Furthermore, the people of this region must find the ambition to further the scope of their intellect, that is, of their knowledge of science, art, and literature. The attribution of supreme value to life itself is another value that must be learned, he says. Such values are pertinent to the extent that the person who adopts them gets the impression that he or she is fulfilling deeply held aspirations. Djaït wrote mainly about Arabs, but these observations apply equally to Iranians.

All the same, leisure and work in the MENA are framed and constrained by a powerful politico-religious establishment. Here leisure, the freest of a society's institutions, nevertheless faces daily an array of interdictions on the acceptability of its activities. No wonder, as Chris Rojek (2000) observes, this institution is also a main fount of social change, and those wanting nothing to do with such transformation will be quick to nip it the bud. What is more, the politico-religious establishment has the regulatory and military power to make this happen.

So, is it possible to regard leisure, work, and community as a main solution to the malaise currently being experienced by the authors of the Arab Spring? That the three are even being proposed as capable of filling this role may appear to some readers as an outrageous proposition. After all, leisure viewed in commonsense is largely trivial activity. Nonetheless, it is the mission of this book to show that such an image is grossly erroneous and that the proposed solution is at once scientifically sound, eminently workable, and highly attractive to Arabs and Iranians themselves. The solution is nevertheless complicated by the fact that brutal leisure and work appeal to some people in the MENA (as well as outside it), as profound leisure the pursuit of which sometimes constrains violently the pursuit of normal leisure there (see chapter 6). In other words, leisure and work will flourish where they are officially welcome and face tough resistance where they are not, especially where they threaten to foster officially unwanted social change.

Acknowledgments

Irving Horowitz was, before his untimely death in March 2012, officially the chair of the board and editorial director of Transaction Publishers. He also founded this firm some fifty years ago. I often wondered how Irving, as busy as he must have been, could take so deep and personal an interest in my publications with Transaction, which included four books before the present one. Busy or not he found time to comment on each text, one shared theme of which was the vague line separating work and leisure. My first book with Transaction—*Between Work and Leisure* (2004)—got the ball rolling in what was to be an eight-year discussion of the matter. The concept of serious pursuits was born of this ferment (see *The Idea of Leisure*, 2012). And, during the writing of the present volume, Irving let me know that I was slacking off on my commitment to work, so involved had I become in describing and analyzing the leisure scene in the Arabic and Persian Middle East. The boundary between work and leisure is vague in this part of the world as it is elsewhere, and it should not be overlooked. Thanks to Irving's prodding I have interrelated the two more fully than in any of my preceding publications. In this book, as never before, their distinctive character dances beguilingly on a common conceptual terrain.

Thus Hannah K. Jones, editor for this book, got assigned a project of exceptional complexity, at least in comparison with my earlier books on work and leisure. Her careful and expert scrutiny of the text is deeply appreciated. It is also most evident on the following pages.

1

Introduction

This book centers on cultural development in the Middle East and North Africa (MENA), in particular its bearing on the Arab and Iranian inhabitants of that region. By all the accounts that I have been able to examine, the MENA is a region in the throes of a developmental crisis. I do not mean, however, development in every sense of the word. For it is a word with several meanings, sometimes referring to developing natural resources; sometimes to developing the economy; sometimes to developing social capacities, as in art, work, and education; and sometimes to other denotations. Such social development is commonly discussed as cultural development, and it is this concept that forms the subject of this book. Here in the MENA, there is a crisis of cultural underdevelopment.

To avoid misstating the case, let us first be clear about the nature of this crisis. Cultural development in the MENA is at a turning point, where in the minds of the partisans of the Arab Spring something should be done to enhance it. It is not an emergency, however, in the sense that, like a natural disaster, quick action must be taken to prevent further loss of life and property. Cultural development in the MENA is not an emergency, only—and crucially—because it cannot be implemented quickly. The following pages show that such development will happen through cultural change, which typically takes years, even if modern electronic communication may significantly speed up the process.

This book approaches Arab cultural development in an unusual way: from the angles of community involvement and the various work and leisure activities. Most of the Arabs in question are Muslim; some are not, but all live in the MENA. For our purposes, this geographic area is composed of the following regions and countries: the Maghreb (Morocco, Western Sahara, Algeria, Mauritania, Libya, and Tunisia),

1

the traditional Middle East, Somalia, Iran, and the Palestinian Territories. Although many differences exist, the Arabs in these areas share a common Arabic language and an enduring cultural heritage. That said, I acknowledge that other scholars might construct this list somewhat differently, and that there is some disagreement about which countries should be included. My list differs, for instance, from that constituting the Arab League. My justification for including Iran, which according to estimates is only 1 to 2 percent Arab-speaking, is that, among other distinguishing characteristics, it is officially a (Shia) Muslim nation, is geographically part of the MENA region, is united with the Arab nations on their view of Israel, and is heavily entwined economically and politically with several other MENA countries.

Let me also be clear that I do not identity with the conception of the Greater Middle East, or GME, and the underlying political interests and beliefs that led to its creation and adoption during the Bush administration in the United States. Be that as it may, placing these countries under a single heading, whether GME or MENA, tends to mask their different levels of cultural development. To counter this misconception, I will note these differences wherever possible.

Finally, I am aware that the locution "Middle East" is unacceptable for some scholars living in the region; they see it as, in Hassan Hanafi's (2000) words, "Eurocentric." That is, they hold the Arab/Muslim region to be as much a center of the world as any other part of it. This is a view from within, and one consonant with the inherently ethnographic stance of this book, which is to identify the contemporary activities in leisure, work, and community involvement and show how they can be harnessed for the good of the individual and society. Still this book is aimed at audiences both inside and outside that region. To avoid confusing the latter, I will retain Middle East as expressed in the MENA. Moreover, to avoid needless repetition, I will not, from here on, generally qualify MENA with "Arab/Iranian." The uniqueness and centrality of its Arab/Iranian, often Muslim, base will be apparent throughout, without adding this linguistic modifier.

Development through Community Involvement

Chapter 3 centers primarily on the antecedents of contemporary leisure, work, and community involvement in the MENA, and on the historical background of these three as it affects the present cultural developmental crisis. The goal of the present section is to explain what community involvement is and how it fosters cultural development as just defined. Leisure and work are taken up subsequently, and much more thoroughly, in chapter 2.

Smith, Stebbins, and Dover (2006, 52) define community involvement as local voluntary action, where members of a local community participate together in nonprofit groups or in other community activities. Often the goal is to improve community life. This concept, which is synonymous with those ideals of civic, civil, citizen, and grassroots involvement, is broader than that of the political process known as "citizen participation," in that community involvement includes both local political voluntary action and nonpolitical voluntary action.

Leisure and work, to the extent that they are social and done with or oriented toward other people, are a pivotal kind of community involvement. This is perhaps most obvious for the leisure that is undertaken as volunteering, the intent of which is to improve community life in some particular way. Other kinds of leisure and their counterparts in work, though also instances of community involvement, are usually not pursued expressly to improve social life. Thus, musicians in a civic orchestra typically play in it for reasons of personal interest; in general, they want to find self-fulfillment in their art. That they contribute to local cultural life and thereby generate social capital—two kinds of community involvement—are not among their principal goals, if they even realize they are doing this. And, to round out this conceptualization, note that solitary leisure is possible, seen, for example, in the lone guitarist, the collector of such natural objects as sand and seashells, and the reader of novels or poetry. Here community involvement ranges from negligible to nonexistent.

Community involvement, social leisure and work included, is a Western concept, the emphasis of which is on voluntary action with other people in the "community." The definition that fits best the scope of this book portrays community as a "collectivity of people interacting in networks, organizations, and small groups within a more or less definable geographic area where the people carry out most of their daily activities accompanied by a sense of belonging to the collectivity" (Smith, Stebbins, and Dover 2006, 50). These theoretic distinctions are important for this book's argument about the MENA.

It is true that kinship groups, whether nuclear families, clans, or tribes, can engage in community involvement. But, unless such a group constitutes an entire community, this involvement must necessarily benefit the broader collectivity and not just a particular unit of kin.

In those areas of the world where local life is substantially organized along kinship lines (e.g., by tribe, clan), among them the MENA, community involvement leading to community growth, to the extent it exists, occurs outside such formations. Thus, by spanning tribes and other large kinship units, community involvement in collective projects brings together people who would not associate were they confined to their familial circles. Those projects are in principle highly diverse, for example, constructing a community well, putting on a community play, organizing and maintaining a nonprofit grassroots association, and establishing and running a public charity. To repeat, the central point is that, in such involvement, a significantly larger swath of the community than one of its tribes or clans benefits from these activities.

Cultural development by way of community involvement is expedited by the presence of social capital. The latter helps enormously in delivering any number of important community benefits. In addition to the obvious ones—for instance, a new water well, a theater piece, a clothing charity—are benefits that are more intangible (e.g., tolerance, willingness to compromise, respect for others). All exemplify nicely the idea of social capital, which refers to the multitude of connections among individuals, as manifested in interpersonal relationships, social networks, trustworthiness, acts motivated by the norm of reciprocity, and the like. It is used by analogy to the concepts of human capital and physical capital (e.g., natural resources, financial resources) to emphasize that human groups of all kinds also benefit from and advance their interests according to the salutary interconnectivity of their members.

Francis Fukuyama (2001) writes that "the literature recognizes social capital as important to the efficient functioning of modern economies, and stable liberal democracy." Halpern (2005) describes in detail how such capital supports these functions, as well as promoting health and well-being, fostering education, and helping to reduce crime. A low level of community involvement is therefore a paramount disadvantage for countries in the MENA trying to enter and participate in what we will refer to later in this chapter as European modernity, and for those precipitating the Arab Spring.

Three Cultural Obstacles to Involvement

As just observed, kin groups, ranging from extended families to entire tribes, provide some of these social benefits but only for group members. A community composed of several such family-based units, to the extent that their members are unwilling to do outside them what they willingly do inside, will fail to exploit its full reservoir of social capital. Refusal to work for the larger collective good beyond that of kin is a common problem in Arab-Iranian communities, where tribal and familial identifications are strong. Margaret Nydell (2006, 71) writes that "family loyalty and obligations take precedence over loyalty to friends or demands of a job." In practice this means that members of a family are expected to support each other in disputes with outsiders. She says that, in the face of threat or criticism from outside, relatives must defend each other's honor, challenge criticism, and display group solidarity. Philip Salzman (2008) holds that, historically, the coming of Islam had the effect of elevating tribal society to an even higher level of integration than previously attained, without supplanting the central principle of tribal political organization. Islam framed Muslims in opposition to the infidel, thereby preserving the balance of opposition. Besides tribal lineage, affiliation and loyalty also came to be defined by opposition, and this remains true today.

> The basic tribal framework of "us versus them" remains in Islam. The conception "my group, right or wrong" does not exist because the question of right or wrong never comes up. Allegiance is to "my group," period, full stop, always defined against "the other." An overarching, universalistic, inclusive constitution is not possible. Islam is not a constant referent but rather, like every level of tribal political organization, is contingent. People act politically as Muslims only when in opposition to infidels. Among Muslims, people will mobilize on a sectarian basis, as Sunni versus Shia. Among Sunni, people will mobilize as the Karim tribe versus the Mahmud tribe; within the Karim tribe, people will mobilize according to whom they find themselves in opposition to: tribal section versus tribal section; lineage versus lineage, and so on.

Salzman argues that this "structural fissiparousness of the tribal order" undermines social cohesion, that is, cohesion beyond the tribe. Everywhere outside the tribe there is opposition to other groups in the community. "Oppositionalism," he says, "then becomes the cultural imperative," and with this attitude, a communal reference is impossible and the decentralization of nomads a workable arrangement. Moreover, a legal system designed to ensure at the communal level civil peace and settle disputes is thereby precluded.

Additionally, the Arab Spring of 2011 has helped stoke a desire among the Berbers, a minority group in the Maghreb, for a revival of their cultural rights (*The Economist* 2011a). Depending on the country, this involves official recognition of the Berber language, obtaining the right to form community associations, abrogating governmental discrimination, and the like. From the standpoint of community involvement, work, and leisure, this development augurs to engender still more oppositionalism, this time based on ethnicity rather than religion or family. Elsewhere in the region, other ethnic groups have also added to the oppositionalism (e.g., the Kurds in Iraq), as have certain non-Islamic religious sects, and all this spanned with a growing tension between the sexes.

Turning to the second cultural obstacle, which may be titled *corporate weakness*, Timur Kuran (2010) observes that Shariah, the dominant Islamic legal code of the Arab-Iranian MENA, lacks a concept of the corporation, a self-governing entity that can be used to generate financial profits or provide social services. Its closest equivalent in Islam is the *waqf*, a trust set up under Shariah law with the goal of offering particular services for all time. The trustees follow an immutable set of instructions, as they go about running such institutions as schools, charities, and houses of worship. But a *waqf*, unlike a corporation, cannot adapt to changing conditions, and it certainly cannot get involved in politics. Nor, as Kuran notes, can it foster social movements or ideologies. Nevertheless, the MENA Arabic world of today does have some corporations, though compared with the rest of the world, their presence and influence is weak.

The third cultural obstacle is close politico-religious control, referred to in this book by the shorthand of *state dominance*. So named because it is the state that effects most of the control—in the MENA often with the threat or actual use of force—the justification for which is religious (i.e., Islamic), when not based on the secular interests of the ruling dynasty. Through state dominance leisure, the freest of a society's institutions, nevertheless faces a daily array of interdictions on the acceptability of its activities. No wonder, for as Chris Rojek (2000) observes, this institution is also the fount of social change, and those wanting nothing to do with such transformation will be quick to nip it the bud. Leisure leading to possible social change is defined as gravely deviant, a subversive act.

Since these three cultural obstacles bear on all aspects of leisure and community development in the MENA, they will serve as leitmotifs throughout this book, appearing where appropriate to contextualize the discussion at that point.

Development through Leisure and Work

Earlier I briefly mentioned the place of leisure and work in community involvement, but what does that mean in detail? All of this kind of involvement is voluntary action and, as such, it is all also leisure. Consider the following definition: "leisure is uncoerced, contextually framed activity engaged in during free time, which people want to do and, using their abilities and resources, actually do in either a satisfying or a fulfilling way (or both)" (Stebbins 2012, 2). "Free time" in this definition (It is further defined in chapter 2.) is time away from unpleasant or disagreeable obligation, with pleasant obligation being treated here essentially as leisure. We shall see in chapter 2 that devotee work is of this nature. In other words *homo otiosus*, leisure man, feels no significant coercion to enact the activity in question.

The main point to be made about leisure in this section is that it should never be overlooked as a principal source of community development, even though this is exactly what so often happens in scholarly circles. Economics and political science are particularly lax in this respect (see Stebbins [2012, chap. 2]). What is known about leisure from the standpoint of psychology has been described as a "social psychology of leisure" and "a child of leisure studies" (Mannell, Kleiber, and Staempfli 2006, 119). These authors hold that "leisure has all but been ignored by social psychologists in the field of psychology during the past 100 years" (112–113).

Yet there are some very profound reasons why leisure and devotee work may be considered a linchpin, if not *the* linchpin, of cultural development. Elsewhere I set out five of these (Stebbins 2012, chap. 2), which are summarized below.

Leisure as the Precursor of Devotee Work

Working as an occupational devotee is very much like pursing serious leisure (Stebbins 2004, chapter 5). Occupational devotion, which will be covered in greater depth in the next chapter, refers to a strong, positive attachment to a form of self-enhancing work, where the senses of achievement and fulfillment are high and the core activity (set of tasks) is endowed with such intense appeal that the line between this work and leisure is virtually erased. An occupational devotee is someone inspired by occupational devotion. Devotee work is the core activity of the occupation. As for serious leisure, it will be further elaborated on in chapter 2 as well, where it is defined as the systematic pursuit of an amateur, hobbyist, or volunteer activity sufficiently substantial, interesting, and fulfilling for the participant to find a (leisure) career there acquiring and expressing a combination of its special skills, knowledge, and experience. These two are considered in chapter 2 under the heading of "serious pursuits."

Occupational devotees turn up chiefly, though not exclusively, in four areas of the economy, providing that the work there is, at most, only lightly bureaucratized: certain small businesses, the skilled trades, the consulting and counseling occupations, and the public- and client-centered professions. Public-centered professions are found in the arts, sports, scientific, and entertainment fields, while those that are client-centered abound in such fields as law, teaching, accounting, and medicine. Today's devotee occupations actually owe their existence in one way or another to one or more serious leisure precursors. Thus some amateurs become professionals, some hobbyists become small business people, and some volunteers become organizational employees.

So serious leisure and devotee work are much the same, even while the latter, in part because it constitutes all or some of a livelihood, is obligated activity, albeit agreeably so. One crucial condition is that devotee work is fundamentally dependent on the domain of serious leisure. *Bluntly put, without this leisure, the devotee occupations would never exist* (Stebbins 2004, chap. 5). This observation, when it comes to the trades and the client-centered professions, is apparent to most everyone, since they know of the pre-apprentice hobbyist and the pre-professional amateur. But when it comes to small businesses and the public-centered professions, it is, alas, sometimes overlooked. The student-amateur precursors of the former constitute a reasonably visible group, whereas the pure amateur-hobbyist-volunteer precursors of the latter are much less evident. With all the media hype surrounding professional athletes and entertainers, for instance, it is easy to forget that these people invariably come from a leisure background, where they learned about their chosen field and their own taste and aptitude for it. Here is where their occupational devotion first took root. As for the student precursors, it should be noted that some may not be motivated by the amateur or hobbyist spirit but rather by a sense of disagreeable obligation (e.g., "my parents insist that I become a lawyer," laments a student who would rather seek a career in music).

Leisure and Work as Avenues for Self-Development

Leisure and devotee work can be main sources of self-development and, especially, of self-fulfillment. The latter refers to the act or the process of developing one's gifts and character to the full capacity. It is a subjective concept, two major components of which are the leisure career and that of devotee work. Of these two, the first is the more foundational, since as just pointed out, today's devotee occupations actually owe their existence, in one way or another, to one or more serious leisure precursors.

A leisure career is the typical course, or passage, of a type of amateur, hobbyist, or volunteer that carries the person into and through a leisure role or activity and possibly into and through a work role (Stebbins 2007, 18–22). The effect of human agency in a person's career in serious leisure (and, for some, later in devotee work) is evident in his or her self-guided acquisition and expression of a combination of the special skills, knowledge, and experience associated with the core activities. Furthermore every serious leisure career both frames, and is framed by, the continuous search for certain rewards, a search that takes months, and in some fields years, before the participant consistently finds deep fulfillment in the chosen amateur, hobbyist, or volunteer role or sometimes later on, in a variety of devotee work. (These rewards are also discussed in chapter 2.) It should now be clear, the leisure career, thus understood, is a major source of motivation to continue pursuing the leisure or devotee work activity.

Leisure as a Source of Personal and Social Identity

Serious leisure participants tend to identify strongly with their chosen pursuits. With their leisure careers, it is inevitable that they would come to see themselves, usually proudly, as a certain kind of amateur, hobbyist, or career volunteer. True, self-perception as a particular kind of amateur depends on how far into the career the individual has got. Neophytes—serious leisure participants at the beginning of their leisure career but intending to stay with the activity and develop in it—are unlikely to identify themselves as true amateurs or hobbyists. To do that, they must believe they are good enough at the activity to stand out from its dabblers, even while they are comparatively weak vis-à-vis more experienced participants, including, in the case of amateurs, the professionals in their field.

Identity has both a social and a psychological side. Thus a person's identity is part of his personality, which in one sense, is a psychological matter. The individual enthusiast's view of self as an ongoing participant in complex leisure activity (serious and project-based forms) is a situated expression of this personal identity. It is based on dimensions like level of skill, knowledge, and experience, as well as number and quality of physical acquisitions (e.g., good health, collectibles) and lasting physical products (quilts, paintings) stemming from the leisure. So, a young woman might remark to a new acquaintance that she is a skateboarder, but qualify the image she is projecting by indicating that she has only been in the hobby two years. She is a skateboarder and proud of it, but do not look to her, at least just yet, for expert demonstrations of its core activities. This presentation of self to the acquaintance is a sociological matter, however, in that the skateboarder not only wants the other to know about her leisure but also for that person to form an accurate impression of her ability to partake in it.

A person's social identity refers to the collective view that the other people in a particular leisure setting hold these same levels and acquisitions. It is by social identity, among other ways, that the community (including family, neighbors, and friends) places people in social space. So, Ahmed not only sees and identifies himself as a coin collector, but various members of the community also identify him this way. The fact that complex leisure offers a distinctive personal and social identity is central to personal development.

Leisure and Devotee Work Can Lead to High Quality of Life and Well-being

High quality of life, however generated, is a state of mind, which to the extent people are concerned with their own well-being, must be pursued with notable diligence. (Did we not speak earlier of career and agency?) Moreover, high quality of life does not commonly "fall into one's lap," as it were, but roots in desire, planning, and patience, as well as in a capacity to seek deep satisfaction through experimentation with all three forms of leisure to eventually carve out an optimal leisure and work lifestyle. In other words, human agency is the watchword here.

Leisure/lifestyle counselors in psychology can advise and inform about a multitude of leisure activities that hold strong potential for elevating quality of life, but, in the end, it is the individual who must be motivated to pursue them and stick to a plan (possibly generated in collaboration with a counselor) for doing this. Leisure policy can also be developed such that people have opportunities to find a high quality of life. Furthermore the drive to find this level of living helps explain the purchases some people make to facilitate pursuing a serious or casual leisure activity.

What then of well-being? For this book, I privilege the social variety, as opposed to its subjective counterpart. Keyes (1998, 121) defines social well-being as the "absence of negative conditions and feelings, the result of adjustment and adaptation to a hazardous world." For him, well-being, though a personal state, is influenced by many of the social conditions considered earlier or considered in chapter 4 as part of the SLP. Though the relationship is probably more complex than this, for purposes of the present discussion, let us incorporate in the following proposition what has been said to this point in this section: social well-being emanates from a high quality of life, as generated by serious leisure or devotee work or both, with either or both of these being rounded out by some casual or project-based leisure (or both). There will be more about well-being in chapter 6.

Leisure and Devotee Work as the Basis for a Positive Lifestyle

Every period of history has experienced negativity, as manifested in the upsetting problems of the day that people want solved. Meanwhile a number of contemporary problems—some of the most celebrated being terrorism, genocide, global warming, and extraordinary economic decline—seem intractable and negative to the extreme. Yet in many parts of the world, where its inhabitants are not directly affected by such worries (e.g., the rest of India and I worthwhile, a condition that, even if all problems were solved, could never be achieved because positiveness is much more than an absence of negativeness, even though such absence would help focus attention on the first.

Personal development is a positive process in life. Such development happens, in part, by finding and pursuing a career in a work activity or a leisure activity, if not both. We find such careers in devotee work and serious leisure but not in casual or project-based leisure. The central activities of such work and leisure (discussed later as core activities) occupy a prominent place in the lifestyles of devotees and serious leisure enthusiasts. This is a main way that those lifestyles come to be experienced as positive.

Cultural Obstacles to Leisure

Leisure has a great deal to contribute to cultural development—it is a linchpin. But what about the three cultural obstacles just mentioned that appear to bar the way to achieving the latter? Will not Salzman's unyielding tribal/fissiparousness/oppositionalism, the corporate weakness of Kuran's *waqf*, and the heavy-hand of state dominance also combine dramatically to curb the pursuit of serious leisure and possibly that of the casual and project-based forms? A full answer to this question is to be found later in this book, starting with chapter 3. But we need to know immediately if there is any hope. Otherwise why read on?

Yes, there is hope. Working from anthropological research and theory, it has been observed that leisure is a cultural universal (Chick 2006, 50–51). Every known society has leisure, even though it may not be recognized by this concept when talked about in the local language. Yet every society recognizes time away from obligation, be it work or nonwork obligatory activity. If the anthropologists are right in their claim, there is leisure in the MENA. The three obstacles have by no means fully inhibited it.

Furthermore, leisure has enormous appeal, especially when viewed against life's obligations, most of which are unpleasant. (Leisure may also be obligated, but such obligation is, by definition, always pleasant.) With such appeal people will find ways, legitimate or otherwise, of engaging in it. In fact, it is not unreasonable to hypothesize that the more repressive a society, the more important leisure of any kind will become. There it is the only bright light in an otherwise dark existence; leisure (and devotee work) as noted above is the only basis for a positive lifestyle.

One reason for hope is that serious leisure is sometimes a source of social capital. Whereas volunteering has been identified as a pillar of social capital as achieved through civil labor (e.g., Onyx, Leonard, and Hayward-Brown [2003]), the suggestion that the volunteering in question is primarily serious leisure has been recognized much more slowly and by many fewer thinkers. Rojek (2002, 25) has put the case most bluntly: "Serious leisure adds to social capital through the voluntary, informal supply of caring, helping, and educative functions for the community." He goes on to observe that in analyses of the post-work society, as conducted, for example, by Beck and Giddens, "the notion of the leisure society is given short shrift" (30).

But what about the role played by other kinds of leisure? Social capital also gets a mighty boost, as argued earlier, when people from various walks of local community life come together in amateur and hobbyist activities, say, to perform in a civic orchestra or play on a football team, meet monthly to discuss a book or learn about falconry. To understand either the rise or the decline of social capital, also requires knowing, among other things, why people engage in such leisure and how organizational arrangements encourage or discourage their participation in it.

There is a sort of community involvement and generation of social capital evident within the tribal structure of the Arab-Iranian societies. The beneficiaries of such activity are, however, commonly members of the tribe where it occurs. But, with the right circumstances, could not that activity spill over to another tribe or even the entire local community? Some organizational *savoir faire* is there, having been learned through participation in certain kinds of intra-tribal activity. Are there not situations where this knowledge and experience could be generalized to all or a major segment of the larger local community? Is the Arab Spring of 2011 supplying the kind of nutrition needed to nourish such possibilities?

Embracing Modernity

The obstacles to community involvement and the serious leisure pursuits among Arabs are also obstacles to embracing modernity as it has evolved in Europe over the past five hundred years. This modernity, says, Hichem Djaït (2011, xxv, 200) includes the values of democracy, liberty, and ordinary life for ordinary people, as well as rights of men and women and the individual, interpreted as respect for oneself, others, the community, and civic society. Moreover Arabs must find strive to further the domains of their intellect, knowledge, science, and art and literature (xxix). Elsewhere in his book, he points out that modernity includes "the attribution of supreme value to life itself" (198). Such values are pertinent to the extent that the person who espouses them gets the impression that he is "fulfilling his aspirations" (in the language of the SLP that person is finding "self-fulfillment").

We will examine more deeply, particularly in chapters 3 and 4, the concept of European modernity and its place in the stream of Arab, Iranian, and Islamic history. In what remains of the present chapter, I want to consider the possibilities of surmounting the three obstacles in light of the Arab Spring of 2011. My general position is that, in leisure and community involvement, the obstacles will be surmounted earlier, while in the political realm of citizen participation they will be surmounted much later, if at all. Especially concerning the second, the obstacles described earlier by Salzman and Kuran are hardly encouraging.

The Arab Spring (sometimes, although less frequently, called the Arab Awakening) appears to be the linguistic invention of the press.

It began on December 17, 2010, when a street vendor in rural Tunisia set fire to himself in protest of the way the local police had harassed and humiliated him and his business. The incident became the rallying point for a revolutionary movement that a few months later saw the overthrow of Tunisian President Zine El Abidine Ben Ali. The spirit then spread through much of the MENA.

Egypt was among the next hot spots to emerge from the Tunisian upheaval. Protests there began in January 2011 and Egypt's president, Hosni Mubarak, resigned in February. More or less simultaneously, rebellious activity commenced in Algeria, Jordan, Bahrain, and Yemen. The Libyan civil war got under way in February, and what is known as the Syrian uprising started even earlier, in January of that year. There has also been (less cataclysmic) unrest in Kuwait, Sudan, Oman, Lebanon, Mauritania, Western Sahara, United Arab Emirates, and Saudi Arabia. Nor have the Palestinian Territories escaped the ferment. Even Iraq (Arraf 2011) and Iran (Tisdall 2011) have experienced some disturbances motivated by events in the region as they bear on local grievances. Still not all MENA nations have been noticeably affected; notable among them is Qatar.

The social roots of these upheavals are diverse. Lisa Anderson, president of the American University in Cairo, describes them for Tunisia, Egypt, and Libya:

> The demonstrations in Tunisia spiraled toward the capital from the neglected rural areas, finding common cause with a once powerful but much repressed labor movement. In Egypt, by contrast, urbane and cosmopolitan young people in the major cities organized the uprisings. Meanwhile, in Libya, ragtag bands of armed rebels in the eastern provinces ignited the protests, revealing the tribal and regional cleavages that have beset the country for decades. Although they shared a common call for personal dignity and responsive government, the revolutions across these three countries reflected divergent economic grievances and social dynamics—legacies of their diverse encounters with modern Europe and decades under unique regimes. (Anderson 2011)

She holds that it is these roots that are of utmost importance and not the spread of the principles of community involvement or the adoption and use of the social media to broadcast ideas and share strategies. These two are merely vehicles for expressing the root grievances, the patterns and demographics of which vary considerably from country to country.

Still use of the adverb "merely" to qualify the role of the social media in the Arab Spring may be inappropriate. If the roots are of utmost explanatory importance as distal conditions, the proximal condition of the highly evolved social media is still critical in explaining the chain of events. That is, without the Internet of today and its universal accessibility, without YouTube, Facebook, Twitter, and the like, would the Arab Spring as we know it today even exist?

Conclusion

The question asked frequently in diplomatic, scholarly, and journalistic circles is what will the "Arab Summer" be like? Will it lead to a blossoming of democracies across the Arab-Iranian MENA? Will it result in more despotic rule, only this time by a new set of tyrants (a reversion to the preceding Arab Winter)? No one knows for sure. Timur Kuran (2011), cited earlier, says the foundations for democracy in the MENA are weak, but that many of these countries do not "have to start from scratch." In other words some private organizations have sprung up, including banks and corporations, and are important as economic pillars. Community involvement and related organizations are examined at length in chapters 5 through 7. Nonetheless, the presence of nongovernmental organizations is strikingly weak. Kuran believes that strong private organizations are needed to help resist totalitarian forces (state dominance), which will have to be reckoned with for some time to come. Our earlier discussion about the strength of kinship ties squares with this possibility.

In line with Anderson's observations, an Arab Summer, as opposed to an Arab Winter, will take different forms in different countries in the MENA, if in fact, Summer ever arrives. Will Winter eventually return in Libya with its "ragtag bands" and tribal and regional cleavages? Will Summer be the more probable cultural season in Egypt with its urbane, cosmopolitan young people? Then there is, for yet another example, Yemen:

> Whether or not Mr. Saleh is forced from power, the political crisis in Yemen will likely remain acute, not only because of its tribal culture and topography, but also because of its deep poverty, high illiteracy and birth rates, and deeply entrenched government corruption. Its economy is precariously tied to oil resources, which are declining rapidly. (*New York Times* 2011)

Furthermore, the country is at present deeply divided between its more developed coastal regions in the south and southwest where the Sunni majority lives and the Shiite mountainous north. The latter, where there is a deep distrust of their national government, is also a sanctuary for a number of Al Qaeda militants. Says the *New York Times:* "The tribes there tend to regularly switch sides, making it difficult to depend on them for information about Al Qaeda. 'My state is anyone who fills my pocket with money,' goes one old tribal motto." It would be hard to predict an Arab Summer in such a place, however fierce and spirited the rebellious events of Spring.

The content of the *Arab Human Development Report 2002* (United Nations Development Program 2002) is consistent with this scenario. This report was prepared by a team of Arab scholars, with the advice from a panel of distinguished policymakers in the region. It acknowledges "significant" progress in development during the three decades preceding its publication, but simultaneously signals three critical deficits (see pages 27–32). There remains a deficit of freedom and respect for human rights, which are essential bricks in the foundation of effective government. Additionally, women are yet to be properly empowered. They must be given every opportunity to build their capabilities and to express them, in the terminology of this book, to find self-fulfillment. Third, knowledge and its use to build a productive society and generate well-being are seriously lacking. The Arab countries rank last of the seven world regions on these deficits (except on the gender employment measure, where they rank slightly ahead of the last-ranked Sub-Saharan countries).These deficits become even more vital in face of the fact that the generation of young Arabs has never been larger than at the present time. The United Nations' report also shows this generation, compared with older adults, is particularly concerned about opportunities in education and employment.

This report was published ten years ago. Has it had any effect? If the writers cited earlier in this chapter, whose works appeared in 2010 and 2011, are any indication, the answer is broadly no. The advent of the Arab Spring further supports such a conclusion.

So what kind of soil nurtured this developmental crisis in the MENA? To answer this question, we need some historical background with which to frame that discussion. This is the subject of chapter 3. For, if leisure, work, and community involvement in the MENA are presently in crisis, this was not always true. In the Islamic Golden Age

(c. 750 to c. 1258) such leisure and involvement did exist, albeit in a form rather different from that of today. Chapter 4 discusses community involvement and the presence of leisure and devotee work activities in twenty-first century MENA. Before presenting this portrait of the MENA's use of free time in past and present, however, we must look into the leisure theory that helps explain it.

2

The Serious Leisure
Perspective

The serious leisure perspective (SLP) can be described, in simplest terms, as the theoretic framework that synthesizes three main forms of leisure, showing, at once, their distinctive features, similarities, and interrelationships. (The SLP and its empirical support in research are discussed in detail in Stebbins [1992; 2001a; 2007].) Additionally, the Perspective (wherever Perspective appears as shorthand for SLP, to avoid confusion, the first letter will be capitalized) considers how the three forms—serious pursuits (serious leisure/devotee work), casual leisure, and project-based leisure—are shaped by various psychological, social, cultural, and historical conditions. Each form serves as a conceptual umbrella for a range of types of related activities. That the Perspective takes its name from the first of these should, in no way, suggest that it be regarded, in some abstract sense, as the most important or superior of the three. Rather the Perspective is so titled, simply because it got its start in the study of serious leisure; such leisure is, strictly from the standpoint of intellectual invention, the godfather of the other two. Furthermore serious leisure has become the bench mark from which analyses of casual and project-based leisure have often been undertaken. So naming the Perspective after the first, facilitates intellectual recognition; it keeps the idea in familiar territory for all concerned.

My research findings and theoretic musings over the past thirty-nine years have nevertheless evolved and coalesced into a typological map of the world of leisure. (For a brief history of the Perspective, see the history page at www.seriousleisure.net, or for a longer version, see Stebbins [2007, chap. 6].) That is, so far as known at present, all leisure (at least in Western society) can be classified according to one of the three forms and their several types and subtypes. More precisely the SLP offers a classification and explanation of all leisure activities and experiences, as these two are framed in the social psychological, structural, cultural, geographical, and historical conditions in which each activity and accompanying experience take place. Figure 2.1 portrays the typological structure of the Perspective.

Figure 2.1
The Serious Leisure Perspective

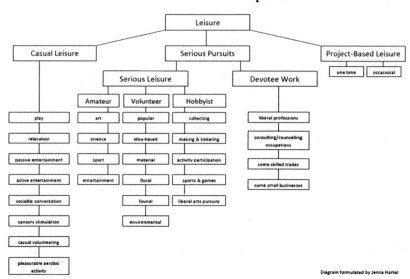

Diagram formulated by Jenna Hartel

Serious Pursuits

In chapter 1 serious leisure and devotee work were placed under the heading of serious pursuits, as its two types. The present chapter further explains this classificatory change, from what was a separation of the two as leisure and work, respectively, to this point in the history of the SLP. The justification for this change is simple: devotee work is essentially leisure. So we should call this spade a spade and explore it as part of the Perspective.

Serious Leisure

Serious leisure, one of the two types of serious pursuit, is the systematic pursuit of an amateur, hobbyist, or volunteer activity sufficiently substantial, interesting, and fulfilling for the participant to find a (leisure) career there acquiring and expressing a combination of its special skills, knowledge, and experience. I coined the term (Stebbins 1982) to express the way the people I interviewed and observed viewed the importance of these three kinds of activity in their everyday lives. The adjective "serious" (a word my research respondents often used) embodies such qualities as earnestness, sincerity, importance, and carefulness, rather than gravity, solemnity, joylessness, distress, and anxiety. Although the second set of terms occasionally describes serious leisure events, they are uncharacteristic of them and fail to nullify, or in many cases, even dilute, the overall fulfillment gained by the participants. The idea of "career" in this definition follows sociological tradition, where careers are seen as available in all substantial, complex roles, including those in leisure. Finally, as we shall see shortly, serious leisure is distinct from casual leisure and project-based leisure.

Amateurs are found in art, science, sport, and entertainment, where they are invariably linked in a variety of ways with professional counterparts. The two can be distinguished descriptively in that the activity in question constitutes a livelihood for professionals but not amateurs. Furthermore, most professionals work full-time at the activity, whereas all amateurs pursue it part-time. The part-time professionals in art and entertainment complicate this picture; although they work part-time, their work is judged by other professionals and by amateurs as being of professional quality. Amateurs and professionals are locked in and therefore defined by a system of relations linking them and their publics—the "professional-amateur-public system," or P-A-P system, which is discussed in more detail in Stebbins (2007, 6–8). But note here that enactment of the core activity by the professionals in a particular field, to influence amateurs there, must be sufficiently visible to those amateurs. If the amateurs, in general, have no idea of the prowess of their professional counterparts, the latter become irrelevant as role models, and the leisure side of the activity remains at a hobbyist level.

Hobbyists lack this professional alter ego, suggesting that, historically, all amateurs were hobbyists before their fields professionalized. Both types are drawn to their leisure pursuits significantly more by self-interest than by altruism, whereas volunteers engage in activities requiring a more or less equal blend of these two motives. Hobbyists may be classified in five types: collectors, makers and tinkerers, non-competitive activity participants (e.g., fishing, hiking, orienteering), hobbyist sports and games (e.g., ultimate Frisbee, croquet, gin rummy), and the liberal arts hobbies.

The liberal arts hobbyists are enamored of the systematic acquisition of knowledge for its own sake. Many of them accomplish this by reading voraciously in a field of art, sport, cuisine, language, culture, history, science, philosophy, politics, or literature (Stebbins 1994a). But some of them go beyond this to expand their knowledge still further through cultural tourism, documentary videos, television programs, and similar resources. Although the matter has yet to be studied through research, it is theoretically possible to separate buffs from consumers in the liberal arts hobbies of sport, cuisine, and the fine and entertainment arts. Some people—call them *consumers*—more or less uncritically consume restaurant fare, sports events, or displays of art (concerts, shows, exhibitions) as pure entertainment and sensory stimulation (casual leisure), whereas others—call them *buffs*—participate in these same situations as more or less knowledgeable experts, as serious leisure. (For more on this distinction, see Stebbins [2002, chap. 5].) The ever rarer Renaissance man of our day may also be classified here, even though such people avoid specializing in one field of learning, choosing to acquire, instead, a somewhat more superficial knowledge of a variety of fields. Being broadly well-read is a (liberal arts) hobby of its own.

What have been referred to as "the nature-challenge activities" (Davidson and Stebbins 2011) fall primarily under the hobbyist heading of noncompetitive, rule-based activity participation. True, actual competitions are sometimes held in, for instance, snowboarding, kayaking, and mountain biking (e.g., fastest time over a particular course), but mostly beating nature is thrill enough. Moreover, other nature hobbies exist, which are also challenging, but in very different ways. Some, most notably fishing and hunting, in essence exploit the natural environment. Still others center on appreciation of the outdoors, among them hiking, backpacking, bird-watching, and horseback riding.

Smith, Stebbins, and Dover (2006, 239–240) define *volunteer*—whether economic or volitional—as someone who performs, even for a short period of time, volunteer work in either an informal or a formal setting. It is through volunteer work that this person provides a service or benefit to one or more individuals (outside that person's family), usually receiving no pay, even though people serving in volunteer programs are sometimes compensated for out-of-pocket expenses. Moreover, in the field of nonprofit studies, since no volunteer work is involved, giving (of, say, blood, money, clothing), as an altruistic act, is not considered volunteering. Meanwhile, in the typical case, volunteers who are altruistically providing a service or benefit to others are themselves also benefiting from various rewards experienced during this process (e.g., pleasant social interaction, self-enriching experiences, sense of contributing to nonprofit group success). In other words, volunteering is motivated by two basic attitudes: altruism *and* self-interest.

The conception of volunteering that squares best with the idea of leisure revolves, in significant part, around a central subjective motivational question: Do volunteers feel they are engaging in an enjoyable (casual leisure), fulfilling (serious leisure), or enjoyable or fulfilling (project-based leisure) core activity that they have had the option to accept or reject on their own terms? A key element in the leisure conception of volunteering is the felt absence of coercion, moral or otherwise, to participate in the volunteer activity (Stebbins 1996c), an element that, in "marginal volunteering" (Stebbins 2001d) may be experienced in degrees, as more or less coercive. The reigning conception of volunteering in nonprofit sector research is not that of volunteering as leisure, but rather volunteering as unpaid work. The first—an *economic* conception—defines volunteering as the absence of payment as livelihood, whether in money or in kind. This definition, for the most part, leaves unanswered the messy question of motivation that is so crucial to the second, positive sociological, definition, which is a *volitional* conception.

Volitionally speaking, volunteer activities are motivated, in part, by one of six types of interest in activities involving (1) people, (2) ideas, (3) things, (4) flora, (5) fauna, or (6) the natural environment (Stebbins 2007b). Each type, or combination of types, offers its volunteers an opportunity to pursue, through an altruistic activity, a particular kind of interest. Thus, volunteers interested in working with certain ideas are attracted to idea-based volunteering, while those interested in certain kinds of animals are attracted to faunal volunteering. Interest forms the first dimension of a typology of volunteers and volunteering.

But, since volunteers and volunteering cannot be explained by interest alone, a second dimension is needed. This is supplied by the SLP and its three forms. This Perspective, as already noted, sets out the motivational and contextual (sociocultural, historical) foundation of the three. The intersections of these two dimensions produce eighteen

23

types of volunteers and volunteering, exemplified in idea-based serious leisure volunteers, material casual leisure volunteering (working with things), and environmental project-based volunteering (see Table 2.1).

Table 2.1
Types of Volunteers and Volunteering

Leisure Interest	Type of Volunteer		
	Serious Leisure (SL)	Casual Leisure (CL)	Project-Based Leisure (PBL)
Popular	SL Popular	CL Popular	PBL Popular
Idea-Based	SL Idea-Based	CL Idea-Based	PBL Idea-Based
Material	SL Material	CL Material	PBL Material
Floral	SL Floral	CL Floral	PBL Floral
Faunal	SL Faunal	CL Faunal	PBL Faunal
Environmental	SL Environmental	CL Environmental	PBL Environmental

Six Qualities

Serious leisure is further defined by six distinctive qualities that are uniformly found among its amateurs, hobbyists, and volunteers. One is the occasional need to *persevere*. Participants who want to continue experiencing the same level of fulfillment in the activity have to meet certain challenges from time to time. Thus, musicians must practice assiduously to master difficult musical passages, baseball players must throw repeatedly to perfect favorite pitches, and volunteers must search their imaginations for new approaches with which to help children with reading problems. It happens in all three types of serious leisure that deepest fulfillment sometimes comes at the end of the activity rather than during it, from sticking with the activity or from conquering adversity.

Another quality distinguishing all three types of serious leisure is the opportunity to follow a (leisure) *career* in the endeavor. The career may be shaped by its own special contingencies, turning points, and stages of achievement and involvement; in some fields, notably certain arts and sports, the career may include decline. Moreover, most, if not all, careers here owe their existence to a third quality: serious leisure participants make significant personal *effort* using their specially acquired knowledge, training, skills, or at times, all three. Careers for serious leisure participants unfold along lines of their efforts to achieve, for instance, a high level of showmanship, athletic prowess, or scientific knowledge or to accumulate formative experiences in a volunteer role.

Serious leisure is further distinguished by several *durable benefits*, or tangible, salutary outcomes of such activity, for its participants. These include self-actualization, self-enrichment, self-expression, regeneration or renewal of self, feelings of accomplishment, enhancement of self-image, social interaction and sense of belonging, and lasting physical products of the activity (e.g., a painting, scientific paper, or piece of furniture). A further benefit—self-gratification, or pure fun, which is by far the most evanescent benefit in this list—is also enjoyed by casual leisure participants. The possibility of realizing such benefits constitutes a powerful goal in serious leisure.

Fifth, serious leisure is distinguished by a unique *ethos* that emerges in parallel with each expression of it. An ethos is the spirit of the community of serious leisure participants, as manifested in shared attitudes, practices, values, beliefs, goals, and so on. The social world of the participants is the organizational milieu in which the associated ethos—at bottom a cultural formation—is expressed (as attitudes, beliefs, values) or realized (as practices, goals). According to David Unruh (1979; 1980) every social world has its characteristic groups, events, routines, practices, and organizations. It is held together, to an important degree, by semiformal, or mediated, communication. In other words, in the typical case, social worlds are neither heavily bureaucratized nor substantially organized through intense face-to-face interaction. Rather, communication is commonly mediated by newsletters, posted notices, telephone messages, mass mailings, radio and television announcements, and similar means. Unruh (1980, 277) says of the social world that it

> must be seen as a unit of social organization which is diffuse and amorphous in character. Generally larger than groups or organizations, social worlds are not necessarily defined by formal boundaries, membership lists, or spatial territory.... A social world must be seen as an internally recognizable constellation of actors, organizations, events, and practices which have coalesced into a perceived sphere of interest and involvement for participants. Characteristically, a social world lacks a powerful centralized authority structure and is delimited by ... effective communication and not territory nor formal group membership.

25

The social world is a diffuse, amorphous entity to be sure, but nevertheless one of great importance in the impersonal, segmented life of the modern urban community. Its importance is further amplified by a parallel element of the special ethos, which is missing from Unruh's conception, namely that such worlds are also constituted of a rich subculture. One function of this subculture is to interrelate the many components of this diffuse and amorphous entity. In other words, there is associated with each social world a set of special norms, values, beliefs, styles, moral principles, performance standards, and similar shared representations.

Every social world contains four types of members: strangers, tourists, regulars, and insiders (Unruh 1979; 1980). The strangers are intermediaries who normally participate little in the leisure activity itself, but who nonetheless do something important to make it possible, for example, by managing municipal parks (in amateur baseball), minting coins (in hobbyist coin collecting), and organizing the work of teachers' aides (in career volunteering). Tourists are temporary participants in a social world; they have come on the scene momentarily for entertainment, diversion, or profit. Most amateur and hobbyist activities have publics of some kind, which are, at bottom, constituted of tourists. The clients of many volunteers can be similarly classified. The regulars routinely participate in the social world; in serious leisure, they are the amateurs, hobbyists, and volunteers themselves. The insiders are those among them who show exceptional devotion to the social world they share, to maintaining it, and to advancing it. In the SLP, such people are analyzed according to an involvement scale as either "core devotees" or "moderate devotees" and contrasted with "participants," or regulars (Stebbins 2007a, 20–21; Siegenthaler and O'Dell 2003).

The sixth quality—participants in serious leisure tend to identify strongly with their chosen pursuits—springs from the presence of the other five distinctive qualities. In contrast, most casual leisure, although not usually humiliating or despicable, is nonetheless too fleeting, mundane, and commonplace to become the basis for a distinctive *identity* for most people.

Rewards, Costs, and Motivation

Furthermore certain rewards and costs come with pursuing a hobbyist, amateur, or volunteer activity. Both implicitly and explicitly much of serious leisure theory rests on the following assumption:

to understand the meaning of such leisure for those who pursue it is, in significant part, to understand their motivation for the pursuit. Moreover, one fruitful approach to understanding the motives that lead to serious leisure participation is to study them through the eyes of the participants who, past studies reveal (e.g., Stebbins [1992, chap. 6]; Arai and Pedlar [1997]), see it as a mix of offsetting costs and rewards experienced in the central activity. The rewards of this activity tend to outweigh the costs; however, the result is that the participants usually find a high level of personal fulfillment in them.

In these studies the participant's leisure fulfillment has been found to stem from an array of particular rewards gained from the activity, be it boxing, ice climbing, or giving dance lessons to the elderly. Furthermore, the rewards are not only fulfilling in themselves, but also fulfilling as counterweights to the costs encountered in the activity. That is, every serious leisure activity contains its own combination of tensions, dislikes, and disappointments, which each participant must confront in some way. For instance, an amateur football player may not like attending daily practices, being bested occasionally by more junior players when there, or being required to sit on the sidelines from time to time while others get experience at his position. Yet he may still regard this activity as highly fulfilling—as (serious) leisure—because it also offers certain powerful rewards.

Put more precisely, then, the drive to find fulfillment in serious leisure is the drive to experience the rewards of a given leisure activity, such that its costs are seen by the participant as more or less insignificant by comparison. This is at once the meaning of the activity for the participant and his or her motivation for engaging in it. It is this motivational sense of the concept of reward that distinguishes it from the idea of durable benefit set out earlier, a concept that, as I said, emphasizes outcomes rather than antecedent conditions. Nonetheless, the two ideas constitute two sides of the same social psychological coin.

The rewards of a serious leisure pursuit are the more or less routine values that attract and hold its enthusiasts. Every serious leisure career both frames and is framed by the continuous search for these rewards, a search that takes months, and in some fields years, before the participant consistently finds deep satisfaction in his or her amateur, hobbyist, or volunteer role. Ten rewards have so far emerged in the course of the various exploratory studies of amateurs, hobbyists, and career volunteers. As the following list shows, the rewards are predominantly personal.

Personal Rewards

1. Personal enrichment (cherished experiences)
2. Self-actualization (developing skills, abilities, knowledge)
3. Self-expression (expressing skills, abilities, knowledge already developed)
4. Self-image (known to others as a particular kind of serious leisure participant)
5. Self-gratification (combination of superficial enjoyment and deep fulfillment)
6. Re-creation (regeneration) of oneself through serious leisure after a day's work
7. Financial return (from a serious leisure activity)

Social Rewards

8. Social attraction (associating with other serious leisure participants as a volunteer, participating in the social world of the activity)
9. Group accomplishment (group effort in accomplishing a serious leisure project; senses of helping, being needed, being altruistic)
10. Contribution to the maintenance and development of the group (including senses of helping, being needed, being altruistic in making the contribution)

This brief discussion shows that some positive psychological states may be founded, to some extent, on particular negative, often noteworthy, conditions (e.g., tennis elbow, frostbite [in cross-country skiing], stage fright, and frustration [in acquiring a collectable, learning a part]). Such conditions can make the senses of achievement and self-fulfillment even more pronounced as the enthusiast manages to conquer adversity. The broader lesson here is that, to understand motivation in serious leisure, we must always examine costs and rewards in their relationship to each other.

Serious leisure experiences also have a negative side, which must always be assessed. Accordingly I have always asked my respondents to discuss the costs they face in their serious leisure. But so far, it has been impossible to develop a general list of them, as has been done for rewards, since the costs tend to be highly specific to each serious leisure activity. Thus each activity I have studied to date has been found to have its own pattern of costs, but as the respondents see them, they are invariably and heavily outweighed in importance by the rewards of the activity. In general terms, the costs discovered to date may be classified as disappointments, dislikes, or tensions. Nonetheless, all research on serious leisure considered, its costs are not nearly as commonly examined as its rewards, leaving a gap in our understanding that must be filled.

The costs of leisure may also be seen as one type of leisure constraint. Leisure constraints are "factors that limit people's participation in leisure activities, use of services, and satisfaction or enjoyment of current activities" (Scott 2003, 75). Costs certainly dilute the satisfaction or enjoyment participants experience in pursuing certain leisure activities, even if, in their interpretation of them, those participants find such costs, or constraints, overridden by the powerful rewards also found there.

Thrills and Psychological Flow

Thrills are part of this reward system. *Thrills*, or high points, are the sharply exciting events and occasions that stand out in the minds of those who pursue a kind of serious leisure or devotee work. In general, they tend to be associated with the rewards of self-enrichment and, to a lesser extent, those of self-actualization and self-expression. That is, thrills in serious leisure and devotee work may be seen as situated manifestations of certain more abstract rewards; they are what participants in some fields seek as concrete expressions of the rewards they find there. They are important, in substantial part, because they motivate the participant to stick with the pursuit in hope of finding similar experiences again and again and because they demonstrate that diligence and commitment may pay off. Because thrills, as defined here, are based on a certain level of mastery of a core activity, they know no equivalent in casual leisure. The thrill of the roller coaster ride is qualitatively different from a successful descent down roaring rapids in a kayak where the boater has the experience, knowledge, and skill to accomplish this.

Over the years I have identified a number of thrills that come with the serious leisure activities I studied. These thrills are exceptional instances of the *flow* experience. Although the idea of flow originated with the work of Mihalyi Csikszentmihalyi (1990), and therefore has an intellectual history separate from that of serious leisure, depending on the activity, flow can still be a key motivational force there (Stebbins 2010a). What then is flow?

The intensity with which some participants approach their leisure suggests that they may at times be in psychological flow. Flow, a form of optimal experience, is possibly the most widely discussed and studied generic intrinsic reward in the psychology of work and leisure. Although many types of work and leisure generate little or no flow for their participants, those that do are found primarily in the serious pursuits of devotee work and serious leisure. Still it appears that each serious pursuit capable of producing flow does so in terms unique to it. And it follows that each of these activities, especially their core activities, must be carefully studied to discover the properties contributing to the distinctive flow experience it offers.

In his theory of optimal experience, Csikszentmihalyi (1990, 3–5, 54) describes and explains the psychological foundation of the many flow activities in work and leisure, as exemplified in chess, dancing, surgery, and rock climbing. Flow is "autotelic" experience, or the sensation that comes with the actual enacting of intrinsically rewarding activity. Over the years Csikszentmihalyi (1990, 49–67) has identified and explored eight components of flow. It is easy to see how this quality of complex core activity, when present, is sufficiently rewarding and highly valued to endow it with many of the qualities of serious leisure, thereby rendering the two, at the motivational level, inseparable in several ways. And this holds even though most people tend to think of work and leisure as vastly different. The eight components are

1. a sense of competence in executing the activity;
2. the requirement of concentration;
3. clarity of goals of the activity;
4. immediate feedback from the activity;
5. a sense of deep, focused involvement in the activity;
6. a sense of control in completing the activity;
7. a loss of self-consciousness during the activity; and
8. the sense of time is truncated during the activity.

These components are self-evident, except possibly for the first and the sixth. With reference to the first, flow fails to develop when the activity is either too easy or too difficult; to experience flow the participant must feel capable of performing a moderately challenging activity. The sixth component refers to the perceived degree of control the participant has over execution of the activity. This is not a matter of personal competence; rather it is one of degree of maneuverability in the face of uncontrollable external forces, a condition well illustrated in situations faced by some of the "nature-challenge" hobbyists mentioned above, as when the water level suddenly rises on a river or an unpredicted snowstorm results in a whiteout on a mountain snowboard slope.

Viewed from the SLP, psychological flow tends to be associated with the rewards of self-enrichment and, to a lesser extent, those of self-actualization and self-expression. Also to be considered part of the Perspective as well as part of flow theory are the pre- and post-flow phases of flow, recently examined by Elkington (2010). These were discussed in chapter 1.

Costs, Uncontrollability, and Marginality

From the earlier statement about costs and rewards, it is evident why the desire to participate in the core amateur, hobbyist, or volunteer activity can become, for some participants some of the time, significantly *uncontrollable*, and the activity engenders in its practitioners the desire to engage in the activity beyond the time or the money (if not both) available for it. As a professional violinist once counseled his daughter, "Rachel, never marry an amateur violinist! He will want to play quartets all night" (from Bowen 1935, 93). There seems to be an almost universal desire to upgrade: to own a better set of golf clubs; to buy a more powerful telescope; to take more dance lessons, perhaps from a renowned (and consequently more expensive) professional; and so forth. The same applies to hobbyist and volunteer pursuits.

Chances are therefore good that some serious leisure enthusiasts will be eager to spend more time at and money on the core activity than is likely to be countenanced by certain significant others who also makes demands on that time and money. The latter may soon come to the interpretation that the enthusiast is more enamored of the core leisure activity than of, say, the partner or spouse. Charges of selfishness may, then, not be long off. I found in my research on serious leisure that attractive activity and selfishness are natural partners (Stebbins 2007a, 74–75). Whereas some casual leisure and even project-based leisure can also be uncontrollable, the marginality hypothesis (stated below) implies that such a proclivity is generally significantly stronger among serious leisure participants.

Uncontrollable or not, serious leisure activities, given their intense appeal, can also be viewed as behavioral expressions of the participants' *central life interests* in those activities. In his book by the same title, Robert Dubin (1992) defines this interest as "that portion of a person's total life in which energies are invested in both physical/intellectual activities and in positive emotional states." Sociologically, a central life interest is often associated with a major role in life. And since they can only emerge from positive emotional states, obsessive and compulsive activities can never become central life interests.

Finally, I have argued over the years that amateurs, and sometimes even the activities they pursue, are marginal in society, for amateurs are neither dabblers (casual leisure) nor professionals (see Stebbins [2007a, 18]). Moreover, studies of hobbyists and career volunteers show that they and some of their activities are just as marginal and for many of the same reasons. Several properties of serious leisure give substance to these observations. One, although seemingly illogical according to common sense, is that serious leisure is characterized empirically by an important degree of positive commitment to a pursuit. This commitment is measured, among other ways, by the sizeable investments of time and energy in the leisure made by its devotees and participants. Two, serious leisure is pursued with noticeable intentness, with such passion that Erving Goffman (1963, 144–145) once branded amateurs and hobbyists as the "quietly disaffiliated." People with such orientations toward their leisure are marginal compared with people who go in for the ever-popular forms of much of casual leisure.

Career

Leisure career, introduced earlier as a central component of the definition of serious leisure and as one of its six distinguishing qualities, is important enough as a concept in this exposition of the basics of this form of leisure to warrant still further discussion. One reason for this special treatment is that a person's sense of the unfolding of his or her career in any complex role, leisure roles included, can be, at times, a powerful motive to act there. For example, a woman who knits a sweater that a friend praises highly is likely to feel some sense of her own abilities in this hobby and be motivated to continue in it, possibly trying more complicated patterns. Athletes who win awards for excellence in their sport receive a similar jolt of enthusiasm for participation there.

So far, exploratory research on careers in serious leisure has proceeded from a broad, rather loose definition: a leisure career is the typical course, or passage, of a type of amateur, hobbyist, or volunteer that carries the person into and through a leisure role and possibly into and through a work role. The essence of any career, whether in work, leisure, or elsewhere, lies in the temporal continuity of the activities associated with it. Moreover, we are accustomed to thinking of this continuity as one of accumulating rewards and prestige, as progress along these lines from some starting point, even though continuity may also include career retrogression. In the worlds of sport and entertainment, for instance, athletes and artists may reach performance peaks early on, after which the prestige and rewards diminish as the limelight shifts to younger, sometimes more capable practitioners.

Career continuity may occur predominantly within, between, or outside organizations. Careers in organizations, such as a community orchestra or hobbyist association, only rarely involve the challenge of the "bureaucratic crawl," to use the imagery of C. Wright Mills. In other words, little or no hierarchy exists for them to climb. Nevertheless, the amateur or hobbyist still gains a profound sense of continuity, and hence career, from his or her more or less steady development as a skilled, experienced, and knowledgeable participant in a particular form of serious leisure and from the deepening fulfillment that accompanies this kind of personal growth. Moreover some volunteer careers may be intraorganizational, a good example of this being available in the world of barbershop singers when they move from president of their local chorus to a regional post within their national organization (Stebbins 1996c, chap. 3).

Still, many amateurs and volunteers as well as some hobbyists have careers that bridge two or more organizations. For them, career continuity stems from their growing reputations as skilled, knowledgeable practitioners and, based on this image, from finding increasingly better leisure opportunities available through various outlets (as in different teams, orchestras, organizations, tournaments, exhibitions, journals, conferences, contests, shows, and the like). Meanwhile, still other amateurs and hobbyists who pursue non-collective lines of leisure (e.g., tennis, painting, clowning, golf, entertainment magic) are free of even this marginal affiliation with an organization. The extra-organizational career of the informal volunteer, the forever willing and sometimes highly skilled and knowledgeable helper of friends and neighbors is of this third type.

Serious leisure participants who stick with their activities eventually pass through four, possibly five, career stages: beginning, development, establishment, maintenance, and decline. The boundaries separating these stages are imprecise, for as the condition of continuity suggests, the participant passes largely imperceptibly from one to the next. The beginning lasts as long as is necessary for interest in the activity to take root. Development begins when the interest has taken root, and its pursuit becomes more or less routine and systematic. Serious leisure participants advance to the establishment stage once they have moved beyond the requirement of having to learn the basics of their activity. During the maintenance stage, the leisure career is in full bloom; here participants are able to enjoy their pursuit of it to the utmost, with the uncertainties of getting established having been, for the most part, put behind them. By no means do all serious leisure participants face decline, but those who do, may experience it because of deteriorating mental or physical skills. It also appears—though I know not how often—that leisure participants sometimes lose interest in the activity, especially after reaching a point of diminishing returns. They may find the activity to be less fulfilling, perhaps on occasion even boring. It is then time to search for a new activity. A more detailed description of the career framework and its five stages, along with empirical support for them, is available elsewhere (Stebbins 1992, chap. 5; Heuser 2005).

Although this can vary according to where in their careers participants in serious leisure are, I have observed over the years that, at any one point in time, they can be classified as either *devotees* or *participants*, although participants typically greatly outnumber devotees. The devotees are highly dedicated to their pursuits, whereas the participants are only moderately interested in it, albeit significantly more so than dabblers. Devotees and participants are operationally distinguished primarily by the different amounts of time they commit to their hobby, as manifested in engaging in the core activity, training or preparing for it, reading about it, and the like.

This is, however, a rather crude scale of intensity of involvement in a serious leisure activity, a weakness not missed by Siegenthaler and O'Dell (2003, 51). Their findings from a study of older golfers and successful aging revealed that data on leisure career are more effectively considered according to three types, labeled by them as social, moderate, and core devotee. The moderate is equivalent to the participant, whereas the social player falls into a class of players who are more skilled and involved than dabblers but less skilled and involved than the moderates (participants). To keep terminology consistent with past theory and research and the generality of the earlier two terms, I suggest we calibrate this new, more detailed, involvement scale with appropriate, new terms: *participant, moderate devotee,* and *core devotee.*

Recreational Specialization

Recreational specialization is both process and product. As process it refers to a progressive narrowing of interests within a complex leisure activity; "a continuum of behavior from the general to the particular" (Bryan 1977, 175). Viewed as an aspect of serious leisure, specialization can be seen as part of the leisure career experienced in those complex activities that offer an opportunity to specialize to participants who want to focus their interests (Stebbins 2005e). In particular, when specialization occurs, it unfolds as a process within the development or establishment stage, possibly spanning the two (of the five-stage sequence of beginning, development, establishment, maintenance, and decline). Should the participant change specialties, specialization may also unfold within the maintenance stage. In career terminology, developing a specialty is a career turning point.

Devotee Work

The subject of devotee work and occupational devotion was partially covered in chapter 1. It was observed that occupational devotees feel a powerful devotion, or strong, positive attachment, to a form of self-enhancing work. In such work, the sense of achievement is high and the core activity endowed with such intense appeal that the line between this work and leisure is virtually erased. Further, it is by way of the core activity of their work that devotees realize a unique combination of, what are for them, strongly seated cultural values (Williams 2000, 146): success, achievement, freedom of action, individual personality, and activity (being involved in something). Other categories of workers may also be animated by some, even all, of these values, but they fail for various reasons to realize them in gainful employment.

I observed earlier that occupational devotees turn up chiefly in certain small businesses, the skilled trades, the consulting and counseling occupations, and the public- and client-centered professions. It is assumed in all this that the work, and its core activity to which people become devoted, carries with it a respectable personal and social identity within the devotees' reference groups, since it would be difficult, if not impossible, to be devoted to work that those groups regarded with scorn. Still, positive identification with the job is not a defining condition of occupational devotion, since such identification can develop for other reasons, including high salary, prestigious employer, and advanced educational qualifications.

The fact of devotee work for some people and its possibility for others signals that work, as one of life's domains, may be highly positive. Granted, most workers are not fortunate enough to find such work. For those who do find it, the work meets six criteria (Stebbins 2004a, 9). To generate occupational devotion:

1. The valued core activity must be profound; to perform it acceptably requires substantial skill, knowledge, or experience or some combination of these.
2. The core must offer significant variety.
3. The core must also offer significant opportunity for creative or innovative work, as a valued expression of individual personality. The adjectives "creative" and "innovative" stress that the undertaking results in something new or different, showing imagination and application of routine skill or knowledge. That is, boredom is likely to develop only after the onset of fatigue experienced from long hours on the job to the point that significant creativity and innovation are no longer possible.
4. The would-be devotee must have reasonable control over the amount and disposition of time put into the occupation (the value of freedom of action), such that he or she can prevent it from becoming a burden. Medium and large bureaucracies have tended to subvert this criterion. For, in interest of the survival and development of the organization, managers may feel they must deny their nonunionized employees this freedom, and force them to accept stiff deadlines and heavy workloads. But no activity, be it leisure or work, is so appealing that it invites unlimited participation during all waking hours.
5. The would-be devotee must have both an aptitude and a taste for the work in question. This is, in part, a case of one man's meat being another man's poison. For example, John finds great fulfillment in being a physician, an occupation that holds little appeal for Jane who, instead, adores being a lawyer (work John finds unappealing).
6. The devotees must work in a physical and social milieu that encourages them to pursue the core activity often and without significant constraint. This includes avoidance of excessive paperwork, caseloads, class sizes, market demands, and the like.

It sounds ideal, if not idealistic, but in fact occupations and work roles exist that meet these criteria. In today's climate of occupational de-skilling, over-bureaucratization, and similar impediments to fulfilling core activity at work, many people find it difficult to locate or arrange devotee employment. The six criteria just listed also characterize serious leisure, giving further substance to the claim put forward here that such leisure and devotee work occupy a great deal of common ground. Together they constitute the class of serious pursuits.

Casual Leisure

Casual leisure is immediately intrinsically rewarding, relatively short-lived pleasurable activity requiring little or no special training to enjoy it. It is fundamentally hedonic, pursued for its significant level of pure enjoyment. The termed was coined by the author in the first conceptual statement about serious leisure (Stebbins 1982), which at the time, depicted its casual counterpart as all activity not classifiable as serious. (Project-based leisure has since been added as a third form [see next section].) Casual leisure is considerably less substantial than serious leisure, and it offers no career of the sort found in the latter.

Its types—there are eight (see Figure 2.1)—include *play* (including dabbling), *relaxation* (e.g., sitting, napping, strolling), *passive entertainment* (e.g., popular TV, books, recorded music), *active entertainment* (e.g., games of chance, party games), *sociable conversation* (e.g., gossiping, joking, talking about the weather), *sensory stimulation* (e.g., sex, eating, drinking, sight-seeing), and *casual volunteering* (as opposed to serious leisure, or career, volunteering). Casual volunteering includes handing out leaflets, stuffing envelopes, and collecting money door-to-door. Note that dabbling (as play) may occur in the same genre of activity pursued by amateurs, hobbyists, and career volunteers. The preceding section was designed, in part, to conceptually separate dabblers from this trio of leisure participants, thereby enabling the reader to interpret with sophistication references to, for example, "amateurish" activity (e.g., *The Cult of the Amateur* by Andrew Keen).

The last and newest type of casual leisure—*pleasurable aerobic activity*—refers to physical activities that require effort sufficient to cause marked increase in respiration and heart rate. As applied here, the term "aerobic activity" is broad in scope, encompassing all activity that calls for such effort, including the routines pursued collectively in (narrowly conceived of) aerobics classes and those pursued individually by way of televised or recorded programs of aerobics (Stebbins 2004b). Yet, as with its passive and active cousins in entertainment, pleasurable aerobic activity is basically casual leisure. That is, to do such activity requires little more than minimal skill, knowledge, or experience. Examples include the game of the Hash

House Harriers (a type of treasure hunt in the outdoors), kickball (described in *The Economist* [2005] as a cross between soccer and baseball), "exergames" for children (described by Gerson [2010a] as a video game played on a dance floor), and such children's pastimes as hide-and-seek.

People seem to pursue the different types of casual leisure in combinations of two and three at least as often as they pursue them separately. For instance, every type can be relaxing, producing in this fashion play-relaxation, passive entertainment-relaxation, and so on. Various combinations of play and sensory stimulation are also possible, as in experimenting, in deviant or nondeviant ways, with drug use, sexual activity, and thrill seeking through movement. Additionally, sociable conversation accompanies some sessions of sensory stimulation (e.g., recreational drug use, curiosity seeking, displays of beauty), as well as some sessions of relaxation and active and passive entertainment, although such conversation normally tends to be rather truncated in the latter two.

This brief review of the types of casual leisure reveals that they share at least one central property: all are hedonic. More precisely, all produce a significant level of enjoyment for those participating in them. In broad, colloquial language, casual leisure could serve as the scientific term for the practice of doing what comes naturally.

It follows that terms such as "pleasure" and "enjoyment" are the more appropriate descriptors of the rewards of casual leisure in contrast to terms such as "fulfillment" and "being rewarding," which best describe the rewards gained in serious leisure. At least the serious leisure participants interviewed by the author were inclined to describe their involvements as fulfilling or rewarding rather than pleasurable or enjoyable. Still, overlap exists, for both casual and serious leisure offer the hedonic reward of self-gratification (see reward number 5 [self-gratification]). The activity is fun to do, even if the fun component is considerably more prominent in casual leisure than in its serious counterpart.

Notwithstanding its hedonic nature, casual leisure is by no means wholly inconsequential, for some clear costs and benefits accrue from pursuing it. Moreover, in contrast to the evanescent hedonic property of casual leisure itself, these costs and benefits are enduring. The benefits include serendipitous creativity and discovery in play, regeneration from earlier intense activity, and development and maintenance of interpersonal relationships (Stebbins 2007a, 41–43). Some of its costs root in excessive casual leisure or lack of variety as manifested in boredom or lack of time for leisure activities that contribute to self through acquisition of skills, knowledge, and experience (i.e., serious leisure). Moreover, casual leisure is alone unlikely to produce a distinctive leisure identity.

Moreover, my own observations of casual leisure suggest that although hedonism, or self-gratification, is a principal reward here, it must still share the stage with one or two other rewards. Thus any type of casual leisure, like any type of serious leisure, can also help *re-create*, or regenerate, its participants following a lengthy stint of obligatory activity. Furthermore, some forms of casual and serious leisure offer the reward of *social attraction*, the appeal of being with other people while participating in a common activity. Nevertheless, even though some casual and serious leisure participants share certain rewards, research on this question will likely show that these two types experience them in sharply different ways. For example, the social attraction of belonging to a barbershop chorus or a company of actors with all its specialized shoptalk diverges considerably from that of belonging to a group of people playing a party game or taking a boat tour where such talk is highly unlikely to occur.

Benefits of Casual Leisure

We have so far been able to identify five benefits, or outcomes, of casual leisure, but since this is a preliminary list—the first attempt at making one—it is certainly possible that future research and theorizing could add to it.

One lasting benefit of casual leisure is the creativity and discovery it sometimes engenders. Serendipity, "the quintessential form of informal experimentation, accidental discovery, and spontaneous invention" (Stebbins 2001c), usually underlies these two processes, suggesting that serendipity and casual leisure are at times closely aligned. In casual leisure, as elsewhere, serendipity can lead to highly varied results, including a new understanding of a home gadget or government policy, a sudden realization that a particular plant or bird exists in the neighborhood, or a different way of making artistic sounds on a musical instrument. Such creativity or discovery is unintended, however, and is therefore accidental. Moreover, it is not ordinarily the result of a problem-solving orientation of people taking part in casual leisure, since most of the time they have little interest in trying to solve problems while engaging in this kind of activity. Usually problems for which solutions must be found emerge at work, while meeting nonwork obligations, or during serious leisure.

Another benefit springs from what has come to be known as *edutainment.* Nahrstedt (2000) holds that this benefit of casual leisure comes from participating in such mass entertainment as watching films and television programs, listening to popular music, and reading popular books and articles. Theme parks and museums are also considered sources of edutainment. While consuming media or frequenting places of this sort, these participants inadvertently learn something of substance about the social and physical world in which they live. They are, in a word, entertained and educated in the same breath.

Third, casual leisure affords regeneration, or re-creation, possibly even more so than its counterpart, serious leisure, since the latter can sometimes be intense. Of course, many a leisure studies specialist has observed that leisure in general affords relaxation or entertainment, if not both, and that these constitute two of its principal benefits. What is new, then, in the observation just made is that it distinguishes between casual and serious leisure, and more importantly, that it emphasizes the enduring effects of relaxation and entertainment when they help enhance overall equanimity, most notably in the interstices between periods of intense activity.

A fourth benefit that may flow from participation in casual leisure originates in the development and maintenance of interpersonal relationships. One of its types, the sociable conversation, is particularly fecund in this regard, but other types, when shared, as sometimes happens during sensory stimulation and passive and active entertainment, can also have the same effect. The interpersonal relationships in question are many and varied, and encompass those that form between friends, spouses, and members of families. Such relationships, Hutchinson and Kleiber (2005) found in a set of studies of some of the benefits of casual leisure, can foster personal psychological growth by promoting new shared interests and, in the course of this process, new positive appraisals of self.

Well-being is still another benefit that can flow from engaging in casual leisure. Speaking only for the realm of leisure, perhaps the greatest sense of well-being is achieved when a person develops an *optimal leisure lifestyle* (OLL). Such a lifestyle is "the deeply satisfying pursuit during free time of one or more substantial, absorbing forms of serious leisure, complemented by a judicious amount of casual leisure" (Stebbins 2007a). People find their OLL by partaking of leisure activities that individually and in combination realize human potential and enhance quality of life and well-being. Project-based leisure can also enhance a person's leisure lifestyle. The study of kayakers, snowboarders, and mountain and ice climbers (Stebbins 2005a) revealed that the vast majority of the three sample groups used various forms of casual leisure to optimally round out their use of free time. For them their serious leisure was a central life interest, but their casual leisure contributed to overall well-being by allowing for relaxation, regeneration, sociability, entertainment, and other activities less intense than their serious leisure.

Still well-being experienced during free time is more than this, as Hutchinson and Kleiber (2005) observed, since this kind of leisure can contribute to self-protection, as by buffering stress and sustaining coping efforts. Casual leisure can also preserve or restore a sense of self. This was sometimes achieved in their samples, when subjects said they rediscovered in casual leisure fundamental personal or familial values or a view of themselves as caring people.

Project-Based Leisure

Project-based leisure (Stebbins 2005b) is the third form of leisure activity and the most recent one added to the Perspective. It is a short-term, reasonably complicated, one-off or occasional, creative undertaking carried out in free time, or time free of disagreeable obligation. Such leisure requires considerable planning, effort, and sometimes skill or knowledge, but it is, for all that, neither serious leisure nor intended to develop into such. The adjective "occasional" describes widely spaced undertakings for such regular occasions as religious festivals, someone's birthday, or a national holiday. Volunteering for a sports event may be seen as an occasional project. The adjective "creative" stresses that the undertaking results in something new or different, by showing imagination and perhaps routine skill or knowledge. Though most projects would appear to be continuously pursued until completed, it is conceivable that some might be interrupted for several weeks, months, even years (e.g., a stone wall in the back garden that gets finished only after its builder recovers from an operation on his strained back). Although only a rudimentary social world springs up around the project, it does, in its own particular way, bring together friends, neighbors, or relatives (e.g., through a genealogical project or Christmas celebrations), or draw the individual participant into an organizational milieu (e.g., through volunteering for a sporting event or major convention).

Moreover, it appears that, in some instances, project-based leisure springs from a sense of obligation to undertake it. If so, it is nonetheless, as leisure, uncoerced activity, in the sense that the obligation is in fact agreeable—the project creator, in executing the project, anticipates finding fulfillment, obligated to do so or not. And worth exploring in future research, given that some obligations can be pleasant and attractive, is the nature and extent of leisure-like projects carried out within the context of paid employment. Furthermore, this discussion jibes with the additional criterion that the project, to qualify as project-based leisure, must be *seen by the project creator* as a fundamentally uncoerced, fulfilling activity. Finally, note that project-based leisure cannot, by definition, refer to projects executed as part of a person's serious leisure, such as mounting a star night as an amateur astronomer or a model train display as a collector.

Though not serious leisure, project-based leisure is enough like it to justify using the SLP to develop a parallel framework for exploring this neglected class of activities. A main difference is that project-based leisure fails to generate a sense of career. Otherwise, however, there is still a need to persevere, some skill or knowledge may be required, and invariably, effort is called for. Also present are recognizable benefits, a special identity, and often a social world of sorts, though it appears, one usually less complicated than those surrounding many serious leisure activities. The skilled, artistic, or intellectual aspects of the project may sometimes prove so attractive, even if not intended at the moment as participation in a type of serious leisure, that the participant decides, after the fact, to make a leisure career of their pursuit as a hobby or an amateur activity.

Project-based leisure is also capable of generating many of the rewards experienced in serious leisure, and these rewards also constitute part of the motivational basis for pursuing such highly fulfilling activity. Furthermore, motivation to undertake a leisure project may have an organizational base, much as many other forms of leisure do (Stebbins 2002). My observations suggest that small groups, grass-roots associations (volunteer groups with few or no paid staff), and volunteer organizations (paid-staff groups using volunteer help) are the most common types of organizations in which people undertake project-based leisure.

Motivationally speaking, project-based leisure may be attractive in substantial part because it does not demand long-term commitment, as serious leisure does. Even occasional projects carry with them the sense that the undertaking in question has a definite end and may even be terminated prematurely. Thus project-based leisure is no central life interest (Dubin 1992). Rather it is viewed by participants as fulfilling (as distinguished from enjoyable or hedonic) activity that can be experienced comparatively quickly, though certainly not as quickly as casual leisure.

Project-based leisure fits into leisure lifestyle in its own peculiar way as interstitial activity, like some casual leisure but not like most serious leisure. It can therefore help shape a person's OLL. For instance, it can usually be pursued at times convenient for the participant. It follows that project-based leisure is nicely suited to people who, out of proclivity or extensive non-leisure obligations or both, reject serious leisure and, yet they also have no appetite for a steady diet of casual leisure. Among the candidates for project-based leisure are people with heavy workloads; homemakers, mothers, and fathers with extensive domestic responsibilities; unemployed individuals who, though looking for work, still have time at the moment for (I suspect, mostly one-shot) projects; and avid serious leisure enthusiasts who want a temporary change in their leisure lifestyle. Retired people often have plenty of free time and may find project-based leisure attractive as a way to add variety to their lifestyle. Beyond these special categories of participant, project-based leisure offers a form of substantial leisure to all adults, adolescents, and even children looking for something interesting and exciting to do in free time that is neither casual nor serious leisure.

The rudimentary social world that springs up around project-based leisure suggests that this form of leisure has at least two potential ways of building community: One, it can bring into contact people who otherwise have no reason to meet, or at least meet frequently. Two, by way of event volunteering and other collective altruistic activity, it can contribute to carrying off community events and projects. Project-based leisure is not, however, civil labor, which must be classified as exclusively serious leisure (Rojek 2002).

Types of Project-Based Leisure

Whereas systematic exploration may reveal others, two types of project-based leisure are evident at this time: one-shot projects and occasional projects. These are presented next using the classificatory framework for amateur, hobbyist, and volunteer activities developed earlier in this chapter.

One-Shot projects

In all these projects people generally use the talents and knowledge they have at hand, even though for some projects they may seek certain instructions beforehand, including reading a book or taking a short course. And some projects resembling hobbyist activity participation may require a modicum of preliminary conditioning. Always, the goal is to undertake successfully the one-off project and nothing more; sometimes a small amount of background preparation is necessary for this. It is possible that a survey would show that most project-based leisure is hobbyist in character, and the next most common is a kind of volunteering. So far, the following hobbyist-like projects have been identified:

1. Making and tinkering:
   a. Interlacing, interlocking, and knot-making from kits
   b. Other kit assembly projects (e.g., stereo tuner, craft store projects)
   c. Do-it-yourself projects done primarily for fulfillment, some of which may even be undertaken with minimal skill and knowledge (e.g., build a rock wall or a fence, finish a room in the basement, plant a special garden). This could turn into an irregular series of such projects, spread over many years, possibly even transforming the participant into a hobbyist.

2. Liberal arts:
   a. Genealogy (not as an ongoing hobby)
   b. Tourism: a special trip, not as part of an extensive personal tour program, to visit different parts of a region, a continent, or much of the world
   c. Activity participation: long backpacking trip, canoe trip; one-off mountain ascent (e.g., Fuji, Rainier, Kilimanjaro)

One-off volunteering projects are also common, though possibly somewhat less so than hobbyist-like projects. And less common than either are the amateur-like projects, which seem to concentrate in the sphere of theater.

1. Volunteering
   a. Convention or conference, whether local, national, or international in scope.
   b. Sporting competition, whether local, national, or international in scope.
   c. Arts festival or special exhibition mounted in a museum.
   d. Help restore human life or wildlife after a natural or human-made disaster caused by, for instance, a hurricane, earthquake, oil spill, or industrial accident.

2. Arts projects (a new category that replaces entertainment theater, see Stebbins [2011b]):
    a. Entertainment theater: produce a skit or one-off community pageant; prepare a home film, video, or set of photos.
    b. Public speaking: prepare a talk for a reunion, an after-dinner speech, an oral position statement on an issue to be discussed at a community meeting.
    c. Memoirs: therapeutic audio, visual and written productions by the elderly; life histories and autobiographies (all ages); accounts of personal events (all ages).

Occasional Projects

The occasional projects seem more likely to originate in or be motivated by agreeable obligation than their one-off cousins. Examples of occasional projects include the sum of the culinary, decorative, or other creative activities undertaken, for example, at home or at work for a religious occasion or someone's birthday. Likewise, national holidays and similar celebrations sometimes inspire individuals to mount occasional projects consisting of an ensemble of inventive elements.

Unlike one-off projects, occasional projects have the potential to become routinized, which happens when new creative possibilities no longer come to mind as the participant arrives at a fulfilling formula wanting no further modification. North Americans who decorate their homes the same way each Christmas season exemplify this situation. Indeed, it can happen that, over the years, such projects may lose their appeal, but not their necessity, thereby becoming disagreeable obligations, which their authors no longer define as leisure.

And, lest it be overlooked, note that one-off projects also hold the possibility of becoming unpleasant. Thus, the hobbyist genealogist may become overwhelmed with the details of family history and the challenge of verifying dates. The thought of putting in time and effort into doing something once considered leisure but now disliked makes no sense. Likewise, volunteering for a project may turn sour, creating in the volunteer a sense of being faced with a disagreeable obligation, which however, must still be honored. This is leisure no more.

Deviant Leisure

Viewed from the SLP, deviant leisure may occur in either the casual or the serious form. (We have so far been unable to identify any project-based deviant leisure.) Casual leisure deviance is probably the more common and widespread of the two. A review of some of the literature in this area is available Stebbins (2007a, 65–67).

Casual or serious, deviant leisure mostly fits the description of "tolerable deviance" (exceptions are discussed below). Although its contravention of certain moral norms of a society is held by most of its members to be mildly threatening in most social situations, this form of deviance nevertheless fails to generate any significant or effective communal attempts to control it (Stebbins 1996a, 3–4). Tolerable deviance undertaken for pleasure—as casual leisure—encompasses a range of sexual activities regarded by some as deviant, including cross-dressing, homosexuality, watching sex (e.g., striptease, pornographic films), and swinging and group sex. Heavy drinking and gambling, but not their more seriously regarded cousins, alcoholism and compulsive gambling, are also tolerably deviant forms of casual leisure, as are the use of cannabis and the illicit, pleasurable use of certain prescription drugs. Social nudism has also been analyzed within the tolerable deviance perspective. (All these forms are examined in greater detail with accent on their leisure qualities in Stebbins [1996a, chaps. 3–7, 9].)

In the final analysis, deviant casual leisure roots in sensory stimulation and, in particular, the creature pleasures it produces. The majority of people in society tolerate most of these pleasures, even if they would never think, or at least not dare, to enjoy themselves in these ways. In addition, they actively scorn a somewhat smaller number of intolerable forms of deviant casual leisure, demanding decisive police control of, for example, incest, vandalism, sexual assault, and what Jack Katz (1988, chap. 2) calls the "sneaky thrills" (certain incidents of theft, burglary, shoplifting, and joyriding). Sneaky thrills, however, are motivated not by the desire for creature pleasure, but rather by the desire for a special kind of excitement, namely, going against the grain of established social life.

Beyond the broad domains of tolerable and intolerable deviant casual leisure lies that of the deviant serious pursuits, composed primarily of aberrant religion, politics, and science engaged in as appealing work or leisure. Deviant religion is manifested in the sects and cults of the typical modern society, while deviant politics is constituted of the radical fringes of its ideological left and right. Deviant science centers on the occult which, according to Marcello Truzzi (1972), consists of five types: divination, witchcraft-Satanism, extrasensory perception, Eastern religious thought, and various residual occult phenomena revolving around UFOs, water witching, lake monsters, and the like. (For further details, see Stebbins [1996a, chap. 10].) Thus the deviant serious pursuits are, in the main, pursued as liberal arts hobbies, as activity participation, or in fields like witchcraft and divination, as both.

In whichever form of deviant serious pursuit a person participates, he or she will find it necessary to make a significant effort to acquire its special belief system as well as to defend it against attack from mainstream science, religion, or politics. Moreover, here, the person will discover two additional rewards of considerable import: a special personal identity grounded, in part, in the unique genre of self-enrichment that invariably comes with inhabiting any marginal social world.

Youth Deviance

Leisure studies research, such as that of Iso-Ahola and Crowley (1991), shows that boredom in free time is an antecedent of deviant leisure, as when bored youth (the group most commonly examined) seek stimulation in drugs and alcohol or criminal thrills like gang fighting, illegal gambling, and joyriding in stolen cars. The authors were primarily concerned with substance abusers, citing research indicating that these deviants are more likely than non-abusers to seek thrilling and adventurous pursuits, while showing little taste for repetitious and constant experiences. In other words, such youth were looking for leisure that could give them optimal arousal, that was at the same time a regular activity—not sporadic like bungee jumping or roller coaster riding—but that did not, however, require long periods of monotonous preparation. Such preparation is necessary to become, for instance, a good football player or skateboarder.

To the extent that wayward youth have little or no taste for repetitious and constant experiences, then what kind of leisure will alleviate their boredom? Some forms of casual leisure, if accessible for them, can accomplish this, but do so only momentarily. Such leisure is by definition fleeting. As for serious leisure, though all activities do require significant levels of perseverance, not all require repetitious preparation of the kind needed, say, to learn a musical instrument or train for a sport. For example, none of the volunteer activities and liberal arts hobbies calls for such preparation. The same can be said for amateur science, hobbyist collecting, various games, and many activity participation fields. Spelunking, orienteering, and some kinds of sports volunteering exemplify non-repetitive serious leisure that is both exciting and, with the first two, reasonably adventurous.

Yet, the problem here is, rather, more one of lack of known and accessible activities that amount to true leisure, than one of being forced into inactivity or to do something boring. Being coerced suggests to the coerced person that no palatable escape from his condition exists. Thus, he must work, since money for necessities will come from nowhere else, or he must give the mugger his money or risk getting shot or beaten. With boring activities, however, palatable alternatives do exist, some of which are deviant, as we have just seen, some of which are not.

Those that are not deviant must nevertheless be brought to light, which is a central goal of leisure education. But what would leisure educators (including leisure counselors and leisure volunteers) teach to chronically bored youth? In general they should focus not on so much casual leisure but on serious and project-based leisure. (This approach is discussed in Stebbins [2010c].) This is not the last word on the matter.

Deviant Leisure and Social Change

Not all deviant leisure is subversive, and the official interpretation of subversiveness varies, sometimes dramatically, from country to country. Thus, the use of alcohol in the West is only deviant, but not officially so, when habitual, or worse, addictive. In the MENA alcohol use is widely illegal, a proscription inspired by the Qur'an. We will see plenty of examples of subversive leisure in the remaining chapters.

Moreover, leisure is a possible source of social change, some of it minor, some of it major. The first is accommodated by a society within the frame of conventional, acceptable activity. In the MENA today this could include, assuming compatibility with Islam, an interest in online video games, a new form of global popular music, or the thrills of an amusement park. By contrast, major deviance is subversive, as seen in activities that controvert the Qur'an (e.g., gambling, consuming alcohol, men and women dancing together). We shall see in chapter 4 that mixed dancing, despite proscriptions, is catching on. Social change is occurring, and the vehicle is a leisure activity, in this instance a hobby. Deviant political and religious systems fashioned in and followed as serious leisure also hold the potential for being subversive. Past and present interpretive challenges to mainstream Islam fit here (for examples, see Djaït [2011, 163–164]), as does advocating for democracy carried out as a social movement. Both exemplify major deviance, with clear capabilities of generating violent reprisals as manifestations of state dominance.

Conclusion

In sum, leisure is superficial (casual), complex and fulfilling (serious), and intense and short-term (project-based). Much of it is conventional, whereas some of it is deviant. And some of the latter is dangerous enough to the politico-religious establishment to be considered subversive. Yet, one popular image of leisure, taken as a category of activities, is that it is wholly superficial and, by that reasoning, should not find its way into a book on cultural development (Stebbins 2012). Hopefully this chapter has scotched such a simplistic view, thereby setting the stage for an examination from past to present of the MENA's rich heritage of leisure and community involvement. There is ample evidence in the coming chapters of the pursuit of all three forms that constitute the SLP.

3

Islam and the Serious Pursuits in the MENA: A History

Many a fine history has been written about the Arabic/Persian-speaking peoples of the world and about Islam (e.g., Djaït [2011]; Rogan [2011]), the religion that most of them embrace. Such works obviate the need for extensive coverage of these two subjects in this chapter. Instead what must be accomplished here is to paint a portrait of the past sufficient to describe the emergence of the contemporary cultural developmental crisis, giving particular attention where possible to community involvement, the serious pursuits, and the other (casual and project-based) leisure activities.

In doing this, I will not fully follow the logic of the serious leisure basis of devotee work. In other words, the devotee occupations whose leisure origins lie exclusively, or almost exclusively, in cohorts of formally trained and subsequently formally licensed or certified students will not be covered here. Medicine, engineering, law, nursing, accounting, school teaching, among others, are thereby excluded. This decision is strictly practical, one of space. It would take another book to examine properly this leisure-work link in the MENA. A worthy subject, for the link does constitute an important arena for cultural development in this region.

Origins

The Arabic-speaking peoples predate the advent of the Islamic religion, which nevertheless eventually became a dominate feature of their lives. Before this time there were, for example, Arab Christians and Arab Jewish tribes. Today the modern Arab is most likely to be Muslim, but a minority do identify with other faiths, often Christianity. Archaeological evidence suggests that before Islam, the Arabic peoples occupied the Arabian Peninsula. Arabic was one of the several Semitic languages spoken there among a number of nomadic and sedentary tribes.

Islam is believed by many scholars to have emerged in the seventh century in Mecca, Saudi Arabia, pioneered by the religion's founder Prophet Muhammad. (He received his first revelation here around AD 610.) Since Saudi Arabia was an Arabic-speaking society, Arabic (in its classical expression) became the language of the Qur'an, the central sacred text of the faith and verbatim word of God. The subsequent spread of Islam and the Qur'an helped establish Arabic as a common language across the southern Mediterranean area, Sudan, and north from the Arabian Peninsula to Iraq. As part of this expansion, Islam, and with it Arabic, forced its way into what is today Iran. Known at the time (seventh century) as Persia, it had enjoyed centuries of dominance in its region realized through a series of empires and associated family dynasties, among them the Persian, Achaemenid, and Sassinid. The principal religion there was Zoroastrianism, which was however, overwhelmed with the Arab invasion that brought Islam.

Djaït (2010, ix) writes that the Islamic Empire and its celebrated culture lasted, in its central core, from approximately AD 700 to 1200. During this period, science, literature, and religious thought were written in Arabic. Although Persian had become the language of poetry, Arabic remained that of the state and culture in general; it was the language of community life. This was the era of the caliphate: the political jurisdiction of a caliph. The caliphate was the first form of government established under Islam. This government was run according to a constitution, which limited the government's power over its citizens. Nevertheless the caliphs were members of dynasties; they were hereditary rulers whose lineage was traced according to a family line.

The caliphate began to break up in the thirteenth century, though Islam and its basis in Arabic continued. Meanwhile, in the political arena, heretofore marginal states started gaining ascendancy:

> In the sphere of politics, the Arabs have bee a excluded from history, for a very long time. Instead, the Turks, the Mongols, the Berbers, the Persians, and the Caucasians have led the destinies of the Islamic world, a domain that had become politically fragmented. (Djaït 2010, ix)

Popular awareness of being Muslim was vague during these times, which nonetheless changed with the onset of European colonization. Now Arabs had another faith with which to compare themselves. Nonetheless the situation was greatly complicated by Ottoman rule, which ran from 1513 to 1922. During this period, the Arabs were ruled by the non-Arab Turks from Constantinople (today's Istanbul) in a foreign language—Ottoman Turkish, a Turkic language that was, however, heavily influenced by Persian and Arabic. Islam was also the dominant religion of the Ottomans. Since then, and even before, European colonialism combined with the pernicious effects of dynastic rule, power struggles, and rampant corruption, even in democratically inclined states (e.g., Lebanon, Iraq), have thrown a wet blanket over cultural development. At the end of this chapter, we will discuss more about this situation in relation to the Arab arts, sciences, sports, and games.

The Arab Arts down through the Ages

This section explores some of the leisure activities that held some level of appeal among Arabs during the course of their history up to modern times. Since direct historical accounts of such activity are rare, a certain amount of speculation will be necessary. For example, where evidence exists of, say, a particular art or sport, I will infer that amateur participants were involved, if not all the time then at least some of the time. For, as observed in chapter 2, devotee work, which includes the livelihood of artists and athletes, is fundamentally dependent on the domain of serious leisure. Note that there is only sketchy data on Arabic artists, athletes, scientists, and other serious enthusiasts of this period actually making something of a living at their pursuit, and in this sense being professional. Perhaps future research will reveal more on this question.

In the field of the arts we will cover literature, music, calligraphy, dance, theater, and Oriental carpets. The field of textiles is omitted, primarily because it difficult, given the scholarly accounts of this craft, to separate utilitarian from artistic work here, or theoretically put, obligatory activity from hobbyist pursuits and even commercial ones. The same holds for embroidery, ceramics, and other art/craft pursuits.

Literature

All the main arts have found expression in Arabic culture, some of them dating to the pre-Islam period. Poetry was the main literary form and means of communication on the Arabian Peninsula during this period. Roger Allen describes the key place of the poet in Arab history:

> From the very earliest stages in the Arabic literary tradition, poetry has reflected the deepest sense of Arab self-identity, of communal history, and of aspirations for the future. Within this tradition the

53

role of the poet has been of major significance. The linkage between public life and the composition of ringing odes has remained a direct one from the pre-Islamic era—when the poet was a major verbal weapon, someone whose verses could be invoked to praise the heroes of his own tribe and to pour scorn on those of their enemies—through the pre-modern period—when poetic eulogies not only extolled the ruler who patronized the poet but reflected a pride in the achievements and extent of the Islamic dominions—to the modern period—in which the poet has felt called upon to either reflect or oppose the prevailing political mood. In times of crisis it has always been, and still remains, the poet's voice that is first raised to reflect the tragedies, the anger, the fears, and the determination of the Arab people. (Allen 2011)

Notwithstanding the preeminence of poetry, the sixth century is the context within which a genre of literary prose begins to take shape. It was considerably strengthened by the writing of the Qur'an, which it should be noted, also contains some poetry. Down to the present, numerous passages in the Qur'an have had an immense influence on Muslims the world over, for it contains injunctions, parables, instructions, among its many other inspirational features. This text has also influenced many an Arabic writer, past and present, not only for its content, but also for its role as the yardstick of literary excellence.

Whereas modern Arabic literature is available in printed form, in days before the printing press, word of mouth was the main medium of communication. The *imams*, or preachers, spread information and religious messages from their pulpits in the mosques, while in the marketplace (suq) ordinary Arabs gossiped and otherwise spread beliefs and opinions of interest within their social networks. This may be seen in leisure studies terms as a main kind of casual leisure (of the sociable conversation subtype), which is still in vogue. Marvin Miksell (1958) reports on the suqs in Morocco that he studied:

> The suq is much more than a market in the economic sense; it is also a social and political assembly of great importance in tribal life. Market day is the time for legal transactions and all manner of negotiations. By nightfall tribal authorities have resolved most of the problems of the week. Since the suq serves as a clearinghouse for gossip and news, its attraction is overpowering. (497)

One gets the sense from Miksell's article that the suq also is, and always has been, a wonderful place for "window shopping," another genre of casual leisure, in this case of the sensory stimulation variety

(Stebbins 2009a, 91–92). (Miksell described how women would wade barefoot through snow, intent as they were on not missing their day at the local suq.)

The writing of the Qur'an was a major turning point in Arabic literature. Allen (2000) points out that there was need to establish a coherent, single version of Muhammad's diverse utterances, which could only be adequately met in a written document. This forced a break with dominant Arab oral tradition of the past and reliance on human memory to carry to future generations. Moreover, the Islamic community was growing rapidly in numbers, thereby presenting a challenge to disseminate as efficiently as possible the Qur'anic word to thousands of people in distant places in Africa and Asia. Near the close of the eighth century the introduction of paper from eastern Asia greatly aided this project.

Allen observes that this rapid spread of Islam quickly resulted in a linguistic duality, in which written and spoken Arabic occupied opposite poles of a linguistic spectrum.

> At one end was the language of written communication and Islamic scholarship, which regarded the language of the Qur'ān as its inimitable yardstick; from this belief developed the later critical doctrine of *i'jāz al-Qur'ān* (the "inimitability of the Qur'ān"), which resulted in a written (literary) language that has undergone remarkably little change over the centuries. At the other end was the spoken language of Arabs, which from Spain . . . and Morocco in the west to the Arabian Gulf and Iraq in the east displayed—and continues to display—enormous variety. (Allen 2011)

The historical background of all this is one of tribal, nomadic culture. The arrival and spread of Islam carried this culture far and wide between the seventh and tenth centuries. The literature expressing it sought early on to preserve the values of chivalry and hospitality, while incorporating a love for animals and describing the stark realities of nature. Nonetheless, it could not escape the diverse cultural influences coming from every region with which it made contact.

The tenth century brought political fragmentation to the broader Islamic community in the form of three separate caliphates: the 'Abbāsids in Baghdad, the Shīite Fā'imids in Cairo, and the Umayyads in Spain. Of interest to this book was the fact that such fragmentation worked to the advantage of literature and its writers, for as Allen puts it the "series of petty dynasties provided ample opportunity for patronage at court." Here was an opportunity for professional work for poets and scholars. A set of major invasions between 1258 and 1800 would, notable among them the Christian Crusades and the Ottoman onslaught, would frequently disturb this happy creative arrangement, but Allen argues that the period was not a intellectually barren as many scholarly observers are wont to say (Allen 2011). It was not entirely a "period of decadence."

The nineteenth century onward is considered "modern," in two senses. One, the Arab literati not only gained considerable contact with European literature (e.g., learned about the novel, the short story, and the drama) but, two, they also were stimulated to reacquaint themselves with the classical Arab past. The latter process became background for creative work carried out around contemporary themes. Nevertheless, at the turn of the twentieth-first century, the Arab creative writer was working at a local level under constraining circumstances characterized by limited freedom of expression and religious and governmental censorship. Many prominent Arab authors at that time, Allen writes, had for political reason spent large segments of their life in exile from their homelands.

It is difficult to discern under such circumstances, and with any accuracy, the prevalence of amateur and professional writing, whether poetry or prose, in the modern MENA. Effective censorship through state dominance probably makes it next to impossible to make a living at writing censorable material (unless doing so in exile). Amateurs might fare somewhat better, if for no other reason than that their readership would usually be more limited and therefore less likely to be discovered by the censorious authorities. On the other hand, many of them might well be inclined to find their serious leisure in safer pursuits. After all, in their free time, they do have some range of choice.

Music

In turning to Arabic music we will steer clear here of its technical nature, save to observe that it is complex enough to be qualified as a serious pursuit when played competently as an amateur or professional activity. (For an overview of the technical side of this music, see Touma [2003].) Part of this complexity is evident in the twenty-four-note system of quarter tones, used to create a music that primarily emphasizes melody and rhythm, rather that harmony. Among the main instruments for melody are the oud (a pear-shaped stringed instrument like a lute), kanun (like a zither), rehab (a stringed instrument either bowed or plucked), ney (a flute blown at one end), and violin (adopted in the 19th century). The riq (a type of tambourine) and the dumbek (a hand drum shaped like a goblet) are used to provide rhythm. Use of these instruments sometimes varies from country to country or region to region within the MENA, and there was also variation across history.

Ali Jihad Racy (1992) describes the rise of Arab music. He observes that this art received a significant boost between the seventh and thirteen centuries when Arabic civilization and Islam were at their height in the MENA. Interethnic interaction during this period put the music of Arabia in close contact with the musical traditions of Syria, Mesopotamia, Byzantium, and Persia. The result was cultivation of a new Arab music. It consisted of deep-seated local elements, including the singing of poetical lyrics in Arabic, as well as new performance techniques, new kinds of intonation, and new musical instruments. Persians and musicians from non-Arab backgrounds numbered among the leaders of this new trend.

The appeal of this music was enhanced by Arabic—the language of the Qur'an and the lingua franca of the Islamic Empire. Racy notes further that:

> court affluence and acquaintance with the worldly splendor of con-
> quered empires stimulated humanistic interests and artistic and
> intellectual tolerance on the part of the Arab rulers. In a short time
> court patronage of poets and musicians became common practice,
> in contrast to the antipathy of some early Muslims towards music
> and musicians.[1]

In other words alongside the amateurs in these two arts were some professionals, whose livelihood was assured by their imperial patrons.

Arab music during this period was shaped by two external sources, one being contact with the writings of certain musicians, mathematicians, and philosophers of ancient Greece. Racy (1992) holds that key Greek treatises provided an extensive musical nomenclature, most of it being translated into Arabic. This corpus has been retained in Arab musical theory down to the present day.

The other external source was the medieval West, its influence being felt during the Crusades carried out between the eleventh and thirteenth centuries and during the Islamic occupation of Spain (713–1492). In Moorish Spain, with its wealth and splendor at court, a number of Arab musicians worked under the patronage of the rich. In this situation, while trying to satisfy the tastes of their "employers," some musicians produced new kinds of vocal and instrumental music. This was, as it were, an occupational influence. Racy (1992) describes another, a stylistic influence:

> Moorish Spain also witnessed the development of a literary-musical form that utilized romantic subject matter and featured strophic texts with refrains, in contrast to the classical Arabic qasidah, which followed a continuous flow of lines or of couplets using a single poetical meter and a single rhyme ending. The muwashshah form, which was utilized by major poets, also emerged as a musical form and survived as such in North African cities and in the Levant, an area covering what is known historically as greater Syria and Palestine. In this area, the muwashshah genre became popular in Aleppo, Syria.[2]

During the rule of the Ottoman Turks (1517–1917), Arab music underwent change stemming from contact with Turkish music and musicians. The professionals among the latter were organized in guilds, some of which were gender based and entertained audiences of the same sex. Soon the Arabs were adopting the guild form. Meanwhile they were also taking an interest in Turkish instruments and such musical forms as the music of the Turkish court and religious Sufi music. Some of the professionals of both ethnicities working in the cities played on the zither or the ney.

Lastly, contact with the modern West has brought further change to Arab music, following the Napoleonic conquest of Egypt (1798–1801) and the subsequent cultural and political exchange during the nineteenth century. Thus, Racy describes how Egyptians began appearing in performances on Italian operas presented in Egypt and, more generally across the MENA, how the use of Western theory, notation, instruments, and overall musical attitudes increased.

Despite this variety of outside influences, Arab music retains to this day a certain common ground, seen in, among other features, an enduring link with Arabic and use of various micro-tones more finely divided than the half- and whole-tones on which Western music is based. Racy also identifies Arabic rhythm as an enduring aspect of the music, one that has survived to modern times. This rhythm stands out for it patterns of beats (two to twenty-four or more) and variations in timbre such as achieved by striking a drum head at different places.

Calligraphy

The Qur'an is written in classical Arabic calligraphy, thereby giving this art special religious status (as expression of God's word). Indeed, historically, the calligrapher strived with his art to find the absolute, his aim being to explore the sense of truth through infinite movement. He believed that he would thereby go beyond the mundane world to achieve union with God. Alia Hassan says that:

> knowledge and literacy have always been emphasized in Islam, especially regarding the reading of the Quran (written primary in Arabic). The ability to read and write in Arabic is almost an obligation to all Muslims and the prolific use of calligraphy demonstrates that.[3]

On a website of the Library of Congress devoted to selections of Arabic, Persian, and Ottoman calligraphy as related to the Qur'an, it is observed that, largely because of the increasing production of Qur'ans, a series of notable stylistic changes were introduced with the intention of facilitating the proper reading and recitation of scripture.[4] The website describes in some detail the changes in script (i.e., toward a cursive style from the earlier geometric styles), in medium (i.e., from parchment to paper), and in form (i.e., toward a more vertical presentation). Along the way a Persian translation of the Qur'an was authorized.

Arabic calligraphy decorates coins, often with short quotes from the Qur'an. It is also an architectural feature, especially prominent in mosques, and it is sometimes incorporated in arabesque motifs. Arabesque is itself an Islamic art form, where the artist assembles repetitive geometric shapes of interlaced foliage or tendrils to create an aesthetically pleasing surface decoration. Additionally Arabic calligraphy came into use in tenth century Persia as inscriptions woven onto silks. The Islamic Arts and Architecture Organization provides a list and short discussion of some of the famous Arabic calligraphers over the centuries.[5]

That there have been professional calligraphers in the past is evident from the existence of works by some of the famous practitioners. That nearly every Arab writes Arabic in calligraphic style does not, however, suggest that most everyone in the MENA is either an amateur or a professional in this art. Wherever in the world it is pursued, calligraphy refers to beautiful, elegant handwriting and to its artistry, not to the penmanship of the ordinary person who uses it for a range of practical needs.

Art

We deal here primarily with painting and drawing, recognizing that the concept of art in the Arab world is much larger and includes calligraphy, decoration, sculpture, and similar expressions. Linda Komaroff, curator of Islamic art at the Los Angeles County Museum of Art, writes that drawings began to appear as accessories of calligraphic manuscripts in the sixteenth century in the MENA.[6] In those days wealthy patrons would hire teams of calligraphers, painters, writers, and allied artisans to produce high-level manuscripts, often consisting of poetry.

Komaroff reports that, by the seventeenth century, a new style of painting had developed at Shah Abbas's court in Isfahan, Iran. She writes, "It was portraiture and it had become prominent. More generic representations than exacting likenesses, such portraits depicted not only sophisticated and refined courtly figures but a variety of other types as well, including mendicants, soldiers, foreigners, and peasants." The State Hermitage Museum in St. Petersburg contains more than four hundred Iranian paintings in various forms (e.g., miniatures, illustrations, oil on canvas) running from the fifteenth through the nineteenth centuries.[7] Starting in the eighteenth century, during the Qajar period, Persian painters began to study European techniques, which brought to the Middle East oil and watercolor landscapes, portraits, portrayals of activities, and the like. More generally, however, depicting human figures in paintings was seen in many Islamic countries as running contrary to the teachings of the Qur'an, constituting thus a confrontation with the machinery of state dominance.

Dance

Irena Lexová (2000) has written a rare scholarly English-language treatise on Arabic dance, in this instance on the ancient Egyptian forms. She observes that dancing was central to ancient Egyptian social life. It took many expressions, from servant girls performing for their royal or simply wealthy masters to farmers celebrating their harvest. These amateur activities were paralleled by professional dancing at ceremonies, celebrations, or funerals, among other occasions. Dancing was done by solo performers, in couples or larger groups, and sometimes it involved soldiers, but it appears that men always danced separately from women. Dancing in ancient Egypt was not a form of exercise or way to socialize, as so much of it is today. It was entertaining, however, or simply expressive of emotions, as in the case of the dancing famers. Much of this can be classified as *rags baladi*, or country dance or folk dance. Lexová writes that the dancing could be gymnastic, imitative, dramatic, lyrical, and at times, even grotesque, and in her book, she describes the diverse movements that constitute each of these as well as their musical accompaniment.

Hala Fauzi is an Egyptian living in the United States; she is a teacher and performer of belly dancing. She has been active in preserving the history and tradition of this form of dance. She points out that "belly dance," a term that is both demeaning and inaccurate, appears to have originated in ancient Egypt, though evidence on this question is admittedly sketchy.[8] "Oriental dance" and "Middle Eastern Dance," she points out, are more accurate labels that avoid simplistically emphasizing one part of the body; the terms accurately serve as a translation of the Arabic *raks sharki*, or dance Oriental. As for "belly dancing," its origins are Western, though here too, it is difficult to be precise about when and where the term first appeared.

Fauzi notes that "dance is so much an integral part of the culture in the Middle East that it is almost like breathing and eating." At the same time it may also be spiritual, in that in ancient times, dances were occasionally performed in temples and sacred places for religious reasons. More generally Egyptians have continued to dance through the ages as a way of expressing different emotions, moods, and as a way to celebrate social occasions, and significant events in their lives, as we saw above with the farmers' harvests.

The Oriental dance, says Fauzi, is now performed more or less throughout the MENA, though unlike earlier, men commonly only do so in private settings. We will return to this dance as a work and leisure activity in chapter 5, where it will also discussed as modern casual leisure entertainment.

Theater

Theater in the form of staged production did not emerge in the MENA until the nineteenth century (Allen 2000, chap. 6). But the region has long had other dramatic traditions, some of them stretching back approximately five hundred years. These are, in the main, the *ta'ziyah* (a passion play involving mourning and consolation in commemoration of the death and martyrdom of the prophet Muhammad's grandson, Hussein), puppetry, and storytelling.

The *ta'ziyah* is a strictly religious performance presented to this day in Shia communities during the Islamic month of Muharram. It is a highly ritualized affair conducted in public. The *ta'ziyah* is especially prominent in Iran, where Shias make up 89 percent of the national population.[9]

The *karagöz*, according to Allen, closely resembles the Punch and Judy show. A sole performer wraps himself in a tent-like structure from where he manipulates hand-held puppets on a stage above him. Different characters come and go, but Karagöz, who is a bumbling, boisterous, simpleton, is somehow always present. He is the hero, chiefly because he puts pretentious hypocrites in their place.

Storytelling in this pre-dramatic period was the province of the *hakawātī* (storyteller). In the 1860s, storytellers in Cairo would accompany themselves on one or more musical instruments, with histrionic gesturing at appropriate points in the narrative (Allen 2000). A contemporary group of Palestinian actors who use the *hakawātī* in several of their plays call themselves the *Hakawātī* troupe.

Theater, as it is understood and presented in the West, took root in the MENA only in the nineteenth century. Allen (2000) writes that Mārūn al-Naqqāsh, a Lebanese business man, returned home from a visit to Italy in 1847 with a play that he had just written. This play—*Al-Bahkīl* (The Miser)—was performed in his home the next year. Much of the play was sung, a formula that was so successful with the audience that it persists to this day in Arabic drama. To perform this and subsequent works in public, al-Naqqāsh had to obtain a decree from the Ottoman authorities. With such state dominance there was bound to be censorship as well, as happened in Syria and Lebanon. The establishment disliked criticism of its policies and women appearing onstage with men, which, according to some, violated Qur'anic principles. Censorship stalled the development of this form of the art, but it eventually gained ground in Egypt in the twentieth century, primarily in cosmopolitan Cairo.

Later in that century, theater companies, many of them Egyptian, began touring parts of the MENA in search of audiences, trying thereby to spread serious theater. Serious theater was translated European dramatic masterpieces or something close to it that was indigenous. Farcical comedy and melodrama, at the popular end of the fine arts

say, a palace or a tomb. Some calligraphers enjoyed a similar existence as compensation for their artistic services. The amateur-student background of these professionals remains a mystery, even though they could not possibly have gained this status without an amateur formation, as described in the preceding chapter. Paul Lunde (1994) discusses the patronage arrangement in the building of the Giralda (construction started in 1172) in what is today Seville, Spain. The chief architect of this mosque, and the man who laid the foundation of the minaret, was Ahmad ibn Basu. He worked in the service of Almohad caliph Abu Ya'qub Yusuf.

A History of Arab Science

The Islamic Golden Age (c.750 to c.1258) is the period during which Arab philosophers, scientists, and engineers contributed substantially to the world of science. In so doing, they worked with the skills and knowledge of the ancient Greeks and Persians, then added their own inventions and innovations to this tradition. Because many of the Arabs of the Golden Age who lived in Mecca were inveterate traders, they were in a position to gain familiarity with innovations from outside their region, for example, the production of paper in China and decimal positional numbering in India. And, because Mecca was also a destination for pilgrims, it served as well as a main crossroads for ideas of all kinds.

Richard Covington, science and history writer for the *Smithsonian, New York Times*, and *London Sunday Times*, among other quality periodicals, has written a lengthy article on the history of Arab science (2007). He starts this piece with a quote from Ahmed Djebbar, a Parisian science historian who was speaking at an exhibition on medieval Arabic science:

> Did you know that the Egyptian doctor Ibn al-Nafis recognized that the lungs purify blood in the 13th century, nearly 350 years before the Europeans?" he asks, standing in front of an anatomical drawing of the human body. Or that the Arabs treated the mentally ill with music therapy as early as the ninth century?

Covington goes on to observe that medieval Arab and Muslim scientists, doctors, and cartographers were "centuries ahead of Europe" in mathematics, astronomy, medicine, optics, cartography, evolutionary theory, physics, and chemistry. The centers for scientific research and experimentation were widely distributed across the Islamic Middle

East, in Baghdad, Cairo, Damascus, Samarkand, Shiraz, Bukhara, Isfahan, Toledo, Córdoba, Granada, and Istanbul.

Present-day Arabs seem largely unaware of this intellectual heritage. This ignorance has prompted Tunisian geologist Mustafa El-Tayeb, director of science policy and sustainable development for the United Nations Education, Scientific, and Cultural Organization in Paris, to issue a warning. He believes that proper recognition of medieval Arab scientific achievements is crucial if Arab and Muslim research is to become sought-after as, in our language, amateur, and professional activity (Covington 2007). In yet another attempt at state dominance, the more reactionary adherents of Islam preach to young Muslims that science is inimical to Islam.

If Arabic was originally a language of poetry and later that of the Qur'an, it also became the language of science. Across the Arab world fellow scientists could read about the ideas and findings of their colleagues however geographically distant. The typical means of conveying correspondence among scientists throughout the Golden Age was by caravan or carrier pigeon.

The ninth century Baghdad mathematician Muhammad ibn Musa al-Khwarizmi is credited with having invented algebra (Covington 2007). His initial motive was to resolve property disputes. Further the ancient Greeks had the erroneous idea that light is emitted from the eye, which the eleventh century physicist Alhasan ibn al-Haitham corrected in Cairo by asserting that light rays travel in the opposite direction, reflecting off the surface of objects to enter the eye. He went on to develop the first rudimentary pinhole camera, or *camera obscura,* demonstrating the tendency in Arab science to be as interested in practical application as in theoretic ideas. The Greeks, by contrast, were more interested in theory than in application. Note, also, that we are indebted to the Arab scholars of this period for the convention of peer review and scholarly citation as confirmation of source material. And this ferment was not limited to the physical sciences. For example, Ibn Khaldun (1332–1406), born in North Africa (present-day Tunisia), is widely recognized as one of the precursors of modern historiographers, sociologists, and economists.

According to Covington the Qur'an stresses the importance of all branches of learning, science included. He cites chapter 58, verse 11: "God will raise up in rank those of you who have been given knowledge." Moreover the value of scholarship among all Muslims is expressed in two sayings commonly traced to the Prophet Muhammad:

"Search for learning even if it be in China," and "The quest for learning is a duty for every Muslim." These aphorisms are consistent with the high regard which the Muslim community has for learning.

According to Roshdi Rashed, a renowned expert on Islamic science working in France, Caliph Al-Ma'mun, who ruled from 813 to 833, had a dream about Aristotle, which prompted him to respect and amass knowledge. His patronage of a select group of scientists was the route to this goal. This relationship became an example for others with sufficient wealth; soon princes, merchants, doctors, and a few well-to-do scholars began funding research through charitable endowments. "Scientists were always close to the courts; there was no such thing as independent science," explains Rashed. "One had to eat and for that the scholars needed a patron, either the caliph, a wealthy merchant or a nobleman" (quoted in Covington [2007]). Here, as in the arts, we may speculate that amateurs existed as well, if in no other way than as students, but it is also clear that such benefactors enabled the full-time pursuit of scientific excellence enhancing the development of pure and applied science across the Islamic world.

The advent of the Ottoman Empire starting in the sixteenth century put an end to the advance of Arab science. Amassing scientific knowledge was not in the interest of these rulers. Their goals were military and organizational, developments necessary to maintain power and privilege.

Sports and Games

Here, as in the earlier sections, we concentrate on leisure/work activity common to much, if not all, of the MENA. Sports pursued in only one or two of these countries are omitted (e.g., rowing on the Nile in Egypt; oggaf, or desert stick ball, in Tunisia).

Gerry Loughran (1972) maintains that sport "is as old as the Middle East." He cites Egyptian wall carvings that depict wrestling scenes in the Pharaonic period. Thus, Dan O'Brien (2000), in a PBS (Public Broadcasting System) program, observes that in 1700 BC, falconry was evident in pictorial records and wall hangings, which showed falconers with birds on their wrists in Arabia and Persia. Falconry has been part of Arab life from at least that date. And, according to the website Equine World UK,

> the Arab or Arabian horse originates from the desert lands of Asia and the most famous are the horses of the Bedouin Arabs, known as

the Original or Elite Arab. Through selective breeding the Bedouins developed an Arab horse which was tough and yet beautiful. It was these Arab horses that were used as a cavalry horse by the Moslems and taken to North Africa and into Spain and France. Many Arab horses were left behind when the Moslems left and were left to breed with local horses creating such breeds as the Andalusian horse.[13]

Then there is the sport of camel racing, which involves running camels at racing speed, rider astride, over a predetermined course. The *Encyclopedia Britannica Online* says it is "limited to running the dromedary—whose name is derived from the Greek verb *dramein*, 'to run'—rather than the Bactrian camel." Historically, and in the present, camels have been routinely used as a mode of transportation and a source of food (meat, milk) and clothing (hide). Camel racing on the Arabian Peninsula—this is the native habitat of the dromedary—dates to at least the early Islamic period of the seventh century. The racing of camels has long been a folk sport practiced in local communities at social gatherings and festivals. Today it is also a professional activity, in which substantial purses are to be won.[14]

Loughran (1972) notes the historical importance of weight lifting in parts of the MENA. In the Lebanese mountains, for instance, village youths traditionally organized weight lifting contests, often hoisting the old *kibbeh* stone, with which their mothers pounded meat and cracked wheat. One may weigh more than one hundred pounds. Wrestling also has a long history in the Middle East, although it, too, has been prominent in other regions of the world. According to the Arabic Wrestling Federation, the first authentic evidence of the development of the sport dates to the Sumerians some five thousand years ago.[15] This organization cites the *Epic of Gilgamesh*, which was written in cuneiform and in which the sculptures and low reliefs combine to reveal the first refereed competitions. They were accompanied by music. There are also a number of historical and archaeological traces of wrestling in Ancient Egypt. Drawings representing four hundred pairs of wrestlers were discovered in the tombs of Beni-Hassan. These drawings, among other sources of information, indicate that corporations of wrestlers in Ancient Egypt, wrestling rules, and refereeing codes existed at the time. The Ottoman Turks gave further impetus to wrestling during their reign in the region. Both wrestling and weight lifting are pursued today as serious leisure activities.

Abdullah Hussaini (1972) writes that association football, or soccer, was probably first played in Arabia in about 1927, one of many products of colonial expansion in the area. He says, however, that it grew fastest after 1939, when introduced on the eastern coast near the oil fields of the Eastern Province of Saudi Arabia. The first players tended to be Aramco employees, who had learned the sport from the British in nearby Bahrain. Craftsmen from Italy, Sudan, Somalia, and Aden who came to work in the area after World War II also contributed noticeably to the rising popularity of the game. Loughran argues that Egypt, which has always been the sports leader of the Arab world in general, is now also a bastion of football. He notes that "they even have women's teams in Cairo, something inconceivable in the rest of the region." Still, with the earliest forms of football being observed centuries ago in some other parts of the world, soccer in the MENA cannot be considered a traditional sport, unlike the others reviewed in this section.

Turning to games, according to the Fédération Internationale de Domino (FIDO), dominoes was and still is popular in the Arab-Iranian Middle East.[16] In its simplest form involving two players, it is a game of chance and, as such, casual leisure. According to the website Chess-Poster.com,[17] the game of chess, was invented in China and reached Persia in the sixth century. With the Arab-Muslim conquest of the Middle East, the game spread throughout the region, eventually reaching Europe by way of the Moorish invasion of Spain in the eighth century. The names of the pieces usually changed upon their introduction to the local culture.

We must not close this section without mentioning the game of mixed chance and skill known as backgammon. John O'Neill (1973) states that no one knows for sure where and when the game originated, but it is clear that, for centuries, it has known great popularity among Arabs. It may have started in India, with its analogue in pachisi, but the Arabs and Persians seem to agree that the game was developed in Persia. Today O'Neill says that "throughout the Eastern Mediterranean region it is unquestionably the single most popular game and in Lebanon, *trie trac*, or *towleh* (table), as it is also called, is practically the national sport."

Conclusion

This chapter has revolved primarily around the serious pursuits, leisure activities on which there is by and large more information than those of casual and project-based leisure. Nevertheless some inferences about the latter two can be made, based on what has been said here about the first. Thus, I noted in the discussion of the suq the appeal of gossip and sociable conversation in general. Another venue for such activity for men, and sometimes women, has been the cafes and hookah (water pipe) bars found in many Middle Eastern countries. Café Riche, a coffee house in Cairo founded in 1908, has always been a stamping ground for intellectuals, writers, and politicians (*The Economist* 2011c). Additionally, there have always been during the typical year in the MENA reasons to celebrate, hold festivals, and mount Ramadan feasts. We just looked into the role of camel races at such events. The racers were, in the past, hobbyists (no professionals in those days), but the spectators were casual leisure participants who were being entertained. To the extent that the celebrations were one-time affairs, or affairs only infrequently carried off (e.g., weddings, male circumcision parties [Price 2011]), those engaged in preparing them, who enjoyed what they were doing, could be regarded as undertaking a leisure project. Daily religious rituals may also be classified as casual leisure, to the extent that they are regarded as pleasurable (on agreeable obligation in leisure, see Stebbins [2000a]).

During the Ottoman period running from the sixteenth to the early twentieth century, it is known that musicians entertained audiences beyond those of the court or wealthy rulers. And Arabic dance, as noted above, has been an omnipresent form of entertainment in the MENA for hundreds years, being considered appropriate for a wide variety of occasions. Since gambling and the consumption of alcohol contravene the Qur'an, both are effectively illegal, even while clandestine pursuits of either or both are bound to occur, especially in the larger cities (Spracklen 2011, 82). In other words, as elsewhere in the world, state dominance in the MENA has produced rules whose violation is deviant leisure (c.f., Becker [1963]), most of which is casual.

But it seems that it is custom, not the Qur'an, which mostly restricts women's leisure, although in modern times some urban women in the MENA are not abiding by the ancient strictures. In general adult and adolescent men and women have traditionally been socially and physically separated. To be sure this does not hold for family relations; here a woman has direct contact with her father, male relatives, and male children. These customs translated into separate educational facilities when, in the twentieth century, females gained access first to primary education and later to increasingly more advanced levels of formation. Daily prayers at the mosque are commonly conducted separately for each sex. In the past women, when they were employed, were legally prevented from being with men in the work place. Still, our treatment of the serious pursuits and casual leisure in this chapter suggests that women are not barred from them so much by law and custom as by taste. At least there is no discussion of females wanting to engage in, for example, falconry, wrestling, or weight lifting. But that taste is changing, as the next chapter will show, and recently, women do dance, play football, and act in theater, although dancing and acting with men has raised many an eyebrow in high political and religious circles.

Nothing was said directly in this chapter about community involvement, chiefly because I could find no historical evidence of it. On this point remember Salzman's assertion stated in chapter 1 that the "structural fissiparousness of the tribal order" undermines social cohesion. There it was stated that concerted leisure as in music, dance, and theater do contribute to social cohesion through a kind of community involvement, but direct contributions of this nature in the MENA seem to have been rare in the past.

In sum, the cultural developmental picture in the MENA as a whole is, as painted in the conclusion to chapter 1, critically in need of some substantial brightening up. In terms of the three deficits noted there, for the majority of ordinary people in these countries—especially the youth among them—the present, unlike the past, offers only a gloomy canvas. But what do the modern patterns of leisure and community involvement look like? Are they as dark as the rest of life?

Further, what can be done in this respect in an area of the world that has for centuries known only dictatorships of one kind or another? What can be done when both the will and the opportunity to learn are seriously effaced? Djaït (2011) points out that:

> as far as learning is concerned, the link with the great old books, has been almost, if not completely, broken. One can therefore postulate that Islamic high culture died around 1500 AD in both its religious and its profane branches (i.e., language, grammar, philosophy, history, and the sciences). The West had nothing to do with this. But within the Islamic world the inspiration for this culture declined for reasons that have not yet been understood. (xxviii–xxix)

The West and its colonial interests have had an indirect supporting role, however, in the unfolding of the awful drama of recent years:

> Over the past 50 years, authoritarian leaders in the region have banded together in support for each other almost blindly, despite all evidence of despotism, totalitarianism and heavy handed oppression.

Although the ideal of pan-Arab unity was never realized, it seems that what has been achieved is a union of corrupt regimes. Grossly misusing the language of Arab unity, they casually dismissed the mass murders that occurred under Saddam Hussein's rule, as well as genocide in Sudan, Syrian oppression of Lebanon, and countless other tragedies. (*The Daily Star* 2005)

One might think that cultural development has no chance in such conditions. Nonetheless, there is in the sphere of serious and project-based leisure and in that of community involvement something to build on in the present. This is especially true in the arts, sports, and hobbies.

Notes

1. From the online version of Racy's chapter available at http://trumpet.sdsu.edu/M151/Arab_Music1.html, retrieved 11 June 2011.
2. From the online version of Racy's chapter available at http://trumpet.sdsu.edu/M151/Arab_Music1.html, retrieved 11 June 2011.
3. Source: http://www.suite101.com/article.cfm/arabic_islamic_architecture/28162, retrieved 12 June 2011.
4. Source: http://international.loc.gov/intldl/apochtml/apocfragments.html, retrieved 12 June 2011.
5. Source: http://www.islamicart.com/index.html, retrieved 12 June 2011.
6. Source: http://www.lacma.org/islamic_art/intro.htm, retrieved 27 August 2011.
7. Source: http://www.hermitagemuseum.org/html_En/03/hm3_5_5_2.html, retrieved 28 August 2011.
8. Source: http://www.gildedserpent.com/articles19/halal.htm, retrieved 13 June 2011.
9. From the website of the U.S. Department of State: Diplomacy in Action: http://www.state.gov/r/pa/ei/bgn/5314.htm, retrieved 13 June 2011.
10. Source: http://islamicart.com//main/rugs/intro.html, retrieved 19 June 2011.
11. Source: http://nazmiyalantiquerugs.com/guide-to-antique-rugs/19th-century-rug-revival, retrieved 30 August 2011.
12. Source: http://www.islamic-architecture.info/A-HIST.htm, retrieved 22 June 2011.
13. Source: http://www.equine-orld.co.uk/about_horses/arab_horse.asp, retrieve d 7 July 2011.
14. Source: http://www.britannica.com/EBchecked/topic/931040/camel-racing, retrieved 7 July 2011.
15. Source: http://arab-wrestling.com/rootsofwrestling.htm, retrieved 7 July 2011.
16. Source: http://www.dominospiel.de/index.php?lang=EN, retrieved 30 August 2011.
17. Source: http://www.chess-poster.com/english/chesmayne/history_of_chess.htm, retrieved 30 august 2011.

4

Contemporary Arab/Iranian Leisure, Work, and Community Involvement

The time has come to examine leisure and community involvement in the MENA of the twenty-first century. A main theme of this chapter will be the fit of the concept of modernity as set out in chapter 1. In this chapter, it becomes a measuring stick. That is, as we go through these pages, we will not only be describing contemporary activities in leisure and community involvement but also examining, as much as possible, which features of them are continuous with the past and which are "modern." The latter are almost always relatively recent imports from the West.

Having devoted considerable space in chapter 3 to the history of art, science, and sport in the MENA, we will open the present chapter with a discussion of these kinds of activities as leisure and devotee work in recent years. Consideration of community involvement follows, which includes some reflection on project-based volunteering. The chapter ends with a look at casual leisure, of which there is a great deal in the MENA of today. Be aware that I will not cover all modern leisure activities—an impossibility in any complex society—but rather cover enough, in sufficient variety, to confirm that cultural development through leisure, work, and community involvement have been possible.

The Artistic Pursuits

In the preceding chapter, I noted Roger Allen's observation that, at the turn of the twenty-first century, the Arab creative writer was working at a local level under difficult circumstances, buffeted by state dominance in the form of limited freedom of expression and by religious and governmental censorship. Today, many prominent

Arab authors have spent large segments of their lives in exile from their homelands for political reasons. Some writers, whose works have somehow offended the theological or political authorities, if not both, have wound up in jail. For example, Egyptian Nawal el-Saadawi has controversial views on women's rights and was imprisoned in 1981 for her books on the subject. Others, writing in praise or at least tacit support of these same authorities, have been given influential positions in cultural organizations.

Allen (2011) describes the content of today's Arab literature. He writes that the movement toward a contemporary literature started in the nineteenth century, fuelled by contacts with the West and a renewed interest in the great Arab classical works. More particularly, after Napoleon invaded Egypt in 1798, an autonomous, Western-oriented dynasty took root, which became a magnet for many Syrian and Lebanese writers. For Egypt at this time offered the freest literary environment of the region, making it the center of the renaissance of this art. When the Ottoman Empire ground to a halt at the end of World War I and independence came to all Arab countries following World War II, the revival spread to them as well.

These sociohistorical conditions gave rise to such European genres as the short story and the essay, as well as some new forms of verse, all fashioned, however, on a foundation of the classical Arab literature. The novel and the drama constituted other imports from the West. It was through translation in the nineteenth century of Western works that these forms became available. Allen states that this renaissance was probably fired by two forces operating in the MENA: the advent of the printing press and the rise and modernization of education. Concerning the first, it "made writing a realistic livelihood and forced writers to abandon the traditional, ornate style of past centuries in favour of a simpler and more direct style that would appeal to a wider reading public" (Allen 2011).

Could this not have been the point at which Arab literary writing moved from being a hobby to being an amateur/professional pursuit and offering thereby a work career for a much larger number of writers than the sporadic patronage arrangements of the past mentioned in chapter 3? Today, even with censorship ever in the wings, professionals exist upon whom amateurs may pattern their own writing style and career in a serious pursuit. Moreover, there is now for the liberal arts hobbyist, a literature on which to develop some expertise as a buff, and for the casual leisure fan of novels or poetry, for example, an available source of entertainment.

Poetry, always a main form of communication in Arab society, became to some extent politicized in a special way following the founding of Israel in 1967. Since then the plight of the Palestinians has been the subject of poetic inspiration, with many of the writers in this area themselves being Palestinian. Allen (2011) notes that some of these poets write about the losses and defiance of their country-men and about their aspirations. Others write to express their com-mitment to revolutionary change. Such literature has buoyed up the reception of poetry in general in Arab society, doing so in face of the powerful attraction in modern times of global communication and of entertainment television, video, and the Internet. Nevertheless, Arab poetry still struggles to find its place in the public domain, Allen says; even though in political crisis, it is the poets who can be counted on to reveal the conscience, pain, and dreams of their brothers and sisters.

Music

It was pointed out in the preceding chapter that, to this day, Arab music retains a certain common ground, seen in, among other features, an enduring link with Arabic and use of various micro-tones that are more finely divided than the half- and whole-tones on which Western music is based (Racy 1992). Arabic rhythm is another enduring facet of the music. The rhythm stands out for its patterns of beats (two to twenty-four or more) and variations in timbre, such as achieved by striking a drum head at different places.

Arab folk music is, today, a main expression of this musical heritage. It varies somewhat from country to country and even from region to region within countries, for after all, such music invariably emerges from local cultural circumstances. Kay Campbell (2007) describes contemporary folk music in Saudi Arabia, which by the way, is often presented as poetry and embellished with song and dance. The 'ardah provides an example:

> The 'ardah is one of many Saudi folk-music traditions that Saudis refer to collectively as *al-funun al-sha'abiyyah*, the folk arts, or more simply, *al-fulklur*, folklore. Varying by region, and again by town and city within each region, individual traditions are known as an art (*fann*) or type (*lawn*). Many combine song with drumming, clap-ping and group dancing. Performers wear regional costumes and

sometimes dance with props, such as the sword in the 'ardah or the bamboo cane in the Western Province's *mizmar*.

Scott Marcus (2006) provides an overview of contemporary *mizmar* folk music in southern Egypt.

Campbell reports that many of the folk arts are thriving in modern Saudi Arabia. Studying them in the evening is a serious pursuit for many youth. Moreover, some of them find an outlet, remunerated or not, in providing folkloric entertainment at weddings. It seems to be expected that a modern wedding party will have a show of this nature. Performers in these troupes may be young or old, if not a mixture of both, and amateur or professional. The appeal of this variety of entertainment, which is flourishing today, spans the age spectrum.

In addition to their love for their folk music, Saudi youth are also enamored of the world music scene (Campbell 1992). Similar to their peers everywhere in the MENA, young Saudis listen enthusiastically to pan-Arab and Gulf-style pop music. It is broadcast via satellite, which carries such networks as Saudi Arabia's Rotana and the Arab networks of LBC (Lebanese Broadcasting Corporation) and MBC (Middle East Broadcasting Center), among others. In their minds there is nothing incompatible about finding both genres attractive. According to Sebastian Usher (2007), in writing for the BBC (British Broadcasting Corporation), modern Arab youth are also rallying these days around a kind of home grown pop music recorded in Beirut and Cairo. The center of this musical revolution at the time were singing superstars like Nancy Ajram and Haifa Wehbe, whose recordings were reaching tens of millions of young people across the Arab world (see also Marcus [2006], on Egyptian pop singer Hakim). Some of this music is sexually suggestive, scraping abrasively against the MENA's conservative religious morality, always risking condemnatory state intervention.

The website entitled Traditional Arab Music (2011) offers an overview of Arabic music, including a brief account of the twentieth-century scene. Arabic pop started to take shape during the 1950s and 1960s, a period during which popular music in the MENA was borrowing certain Western elements, as pioneered by Dalilda, an Egyptian-born singer and actress. By the 1970s, several other singers had joined the trend, and the new music had acquired recognizable features. Arabic pop is usually identifiable by its Western-style songs sung with Arabic lyrics and accompanied by Arabic instruments. Melodies typically consist of both Eastern and Western motifs.

Today, Arabic pop continues to attract a multitude of followers, even outside the MENA and particularly where its expatriates now live in large numbers.

Reggae, hip-hop, and rhythm and blues have, in the past five years or so, also begun to leave their mark on Arabic music. The second commonly involves a rapper being featured in a song (e.g., Ishtar in her song "Habibi Sawah"). More radical, from the standpoint of Arab culture, are those artists who use rhythm and blues and reggae beats to the full, as exemplified in the music of Darine. In Baghdad hip-hop combined with Arabic music mixes Western and Islamic subjects (Arango and Ghazi 2011). Moreover, rap songs in Arabic, spread through the various social media across Arab North Africa, have disseminated ideas and anthems in support of the Arab Spring (Fernandes 2012). All this has provoked mixed reactions, both critical and commercial. None of these forms, however, enjoys widespread appeal. As such none is truly popular.

Arabic Jazz has a following, with many groups playing typical jazz instruments in their performances. Early jazz influences began with use of the saxophone by musicians like Samir Suroor, who presents an Oriental style. Use of the saxophone in that manner is also evident in Abdel Halim Hafez's performances, as well as the more recent work of Kadim Al Sahir and Rida Al Abdallah. The first mainstream jazz elements entered Arab music by way of the Rahbani brothers. Ziad Rahbani, a Lebanese composer and pianist, has also advanced today's Oriental jazz movement, inspiring singers like Rima Khcheich, Salma El Mosfi, and at one point, Latifa.

Rock music is popular everywhere on the planet, the Arab world being no exception. Numerous Arab bands, performing on traditional Arabic instruments, offer hard rock. Traditional Arabic Music (2011) holds that Arab rock is gaining plenty of attention in the Middle East, featuring bands such as Meen and Dabke in Lebanon and bands like Jadal in Jordan.

Ivan Hewitt (2011) says of (European) classical music that, in much of the MENA, it is scarcely visible. He observes that:

> there is a large portion of the globe where classical music barely registers. It stretches from Turkey right down the Arab peninsula, and across Iraq and Iran. Here and there in this vast area you find little pockets of activity. There are long-standing orchestras in Cairo and Beirut and Tehran, and conservatoires in Beirut and Syria. But they are delicate flowers, starved of resources, and liable to be

79

condemned at any moment as corrupt by hard-line Muslim clerics. Even in Turkey, where Western music was encouraged by the founder of the modern secular state, there have been calls to ban Western music such as pop and classical.

In this cultural climate it should be no surprise that Arab composers of Western classical music are rather hard to find. Nonetheless there are classical orchestras: the Syrian National Symphony Orchestra, Cairo Symphony Orchestra, Lebanese National Symphony Orchestra, Iraqi National Symphony Orchestra, Tehran Philharmonic Symphony Orchestra, and others. It follows that leisure and work in this area for Arab amateurs, professionals, buffs, and fans is available, albeit on a limited scale.

Calligraphy

As stated earlier, there have been professional calligraphers for centuries. Of interest in this chapter is the fact that this art form, intimately linked as it is with Islam and the Qur'an, continues to flourish in twenty-first century MENA. Nowadays, many professional calligraphers in this part of the world receive formal training in their art at institutions of high reputation, among them the Faculty of Fine Arts at Damascus University and the School of Improving Arabic Calligraphy in Cairo. In the past, before the establishment of such programs, would-be calligraphers served as apprentices to one or a few established practitioners and, with luck, one of renown.

A living is now possible for professionals, found for example, in making greeting cards, posters, calligraphic prints, and decorative images. Many devout Muslims adorn their homes and offices with calligraphic works of art. Museums and galleries in the MENA routinely offer exhibitions of calligraphic works by recognized artists. And, beyond the professional schools, are the large numbers of amateurs, whose existence is evidenced by attendance at calligraphy schools. Rym Ghazal (2011) has written about Ali al Doury, professional master calligrapher, artist and head of the Sharjah Centre for Arabic Calligraphy and Ornamentation. Ghazal notes that:

> since the centre opened in the emirate's heritage area in 1999, under the patronage of Dr Sheikh Sultan bin Mohammed, Ruler of Sharjah [an emirate of the United Arab Emirates], more than 10,000 students have had a lesson with the 61-year-old calligraphy master from Iraq. They come from all walks of life and all nationalities, signing up for a month-long course of three sessions a week at a cost of Dh100,

with the option of renewing. "Initially, there was more interest from non-Arabs to learn this art, with only recently Arabs are going back to their roots and learning the art and script of their ancestors," Mr al Doury said. Before heading the centre, Mr al Doury helped draft textbooks on Arabic writing for schools in Sharjah back in the 1980s. They helped to address what is becoming a lost art.

Perhaps the art is more alive and well than Mr. al Doury realizes, given the number of students he has taught over the years. Data on the number of fans and buffs visiting calligraphic exhibitions at galleries and museums might further support this hypothesis.

Art

Many museums and galleries in the MENA also offer exhibitions of Islamic and, more generally, Arabic paintings. Nevertheless, as the website Icon-ik observes, there are sometimes problems:

> The crusade in question is the birth of a new art movement being pioneered by a select group of artists and thought-leaders.
>
> The so-called "Art Salon" movement is spearheaded by Kuwaiti fine artist and university Professor Shurooq Amin.
>
> Politics, religion and sexuality are the three main threads of her work, says Amin, who unapologetically pushes the cultural boundaries of society and religion with which she is all too familiar.
>
> Represented by Lahd Gallery, Amin has shown her work internationally, but for political reasons, she often cannot exhibit in her home country.
>
> Amin says her plight is to open up the eyes of the Arab world and she is confident that she can do so without sacrificing her spirituality.[18]

Painting, as with writing and theater, can be the target of censorship.

Be that as it may, it is possible to obtain a bachelor's degree in painting at the University of Damascus and bachelor's and master's degrees in both painting and photography at the University of Tehran. In Egypt Helwan University has a full-fledged Faculty of Fine Arts, which offers degrees in painting, drawing, and photography. Search the Yellow Pages using www.wayp.com and the search term "art lessons." Among others you will find that the Anamel Art Academy in Cairo offers drawing lessons and the Académie des arts traditionnels in Casablanca offers adult education in the various traditional Arab arts. In Amman, for example, children and young adults can choose among the many private and government-sponsored classes in sculpture, painting, and ceramics at the Orfali and Dar al-Anda galleries.[19] Private lessons with local professionals are probably also available in many MENA cities, the availability of which can be determined by inquiring at local galleries and museums.

Meanwhile, at least in Saudi Arabia, government control has declined to the point of permitting in this country a major modern art and stand-up comedy festival (*The Economist* 2012, 49). The content of both arts at this event revolved primarily around controversial issues like religious extremism, cultural conservatism, and the ban on women driving. The target audience of the participants was ordinary people, driven by the desire of the first to precipitate nonviolent social change.

Dance

Hala Fauzi was cited in chapter 3 as stating that the Oriental dance is now performed more or less throughout the MENA, though today, men commonly dance only in private settings. Yet, the practice, at least in Egypt, is regarded as only marginally acceptable. Professionals dance at parties, weddings, and other gatherings, but according the documentary video "Belly Dancers of Cairo," they are often stigmatized as prostitutes (NS Enterprises 2008). In an atmosphere of growing religious conservatism, this attitude has dampened both present-day amateur and professional enthusiasm for the art, because women are supposed to be covered and demure. Nevertheless, they are occasionally asked to perform at the events just listed. In this role they symbolize fertility and joy.

Though our sample of the MENA countries where Oriental dancing is performed is quite thin, it seems reasonable to hypothesize that, in part because of the wide spread traditional religious view of women, it remains an uncommon leisure pursuit. Still, at least in Egypt, there is a fairly robust demand for these dancers, suggesting that professional work as entertainers exists for a number of them.

Meanwhile, the folk dance tradition continues in modern times. Women and men's folk dances are an age-old celebratory tradition. As earlier, both sexes tend to dance in separate groups, sometimes featuring an occasional solo. These dances are usually performed for family celebrations of weddings, religious holidays, national holidays, and more recently, school graduations. The Cairo Opera House also offers the occasional evening of folk dance. Each region, and each town within a region, has its unique dance customs, though they share other, broader traditions (Campbell 1999). Furthermore, Egypt's Academy of the Arts includes the High Institute of Folk Arts, one mission of which is to train performers in music and dance.

In addition Academy has an institute devoted to ballet, established in 1959. Also available in Cairo and Beirut are several dance schools and academies, where it is possible to study this genre of dance. The Cairo Opera Ballet Company, which is affiliated with the institute just mentioned, performs regularly in Egypt (often at the Cairo Opera House) and around the world. In Damascus at least two performance outlets for ballet exist in the Centre Culturel Français de Damas and the Dar-Al-Assad for Arts and Culture. In Casablanca, there is the Ballet Theatre Zion. In other words, in ballet in some parts of the MENA, one finds opportunities for its serious pursuit (as work or leisure) and as a liberal arts hobby (as a buff) and as casual leisure (as entertainment).

Theater

As stated earlier, theater in the form of staged dramatic productions did not emerge in the MENA until the nineteenth century (Allen 2000, chap. 6), but the region has long had other dramatic traditions, and they have a substantial following in the present, in particular, storytelling, the *ta'ziyah* (a passion play described in chapter 3), and puppetry. The *ta'ziyah* continues to be performed during Muharram (in Islam the first of the four sacred months of the year), especially in Iran. Of importance for this book is the fact that the actors are chiefly nonprofessional and energize the audience with their enthusiasm and absorption (*Encyclopedia Britannica*, 1995).

Continuing with staged dramatic productions, we may say that, in general, training and performance facilities are available in several of the capital cities of the MENA. Here is an aperçu. Among the drama schools are the Helen O'Grady Drama Academy Cairo; École de Musique Ghassan Yammine in Beirut (including an actors school); the Performing Arts Center in Amman (offering children, youth, men, and women the opportunity to develop their talents in various performing arts); and the Dramatic Arts Centre in Tehran. Turning to theatrical performance in 2011, the year marked the twentieth anniversary of the Experimental Theatre Festival in Cairo, which features local theater companies. It offers drama troupes the opportunity to perform and exchange ideas through theatrical experimentation using digital media. In Beirut we find the Beirut Theatre, Zoukak Theatre Company, and ImproBeirut, among several others. Theater is also available in Damascus (Damascus National Theatre) and long-standing annual theater festivals take place in Amman, Tehran, and Casablanca, to mention a few. Certain venues in these cities also offer musical theater.

Then there is the theatrical scene in Saudi Arabia, where men are permitted to perform while women's dramatic interests are suppressed. Habib Shaikh (2007), a journalist, wrote that:

> a group of young women in Riyadh have formed a cultural group called "Act" in an effort to energise the capital cultural scene and to create a "real interactive" venue for young women writers and artists.

> According to the founders of the group, Kawthar Mousa, Ahlam Al Zaeam and Yumna Salem, all writers in their 20s, the Riyadh Literary Club's activities are strictly academic and dry, something [that] does not appeal to the younger generation.

> "We aim to mix all cultural activities under the group's umbrella of having short-stories, poetry, drama, photography, fine arts, and even singing and music," said 26-year-old Mousa. She added that real culture is more than just inviting writers for a reading or reviewing a work.

> "We don't want to honour writers by giving them a speech or hosting them once a year. Rather, we wish to activate them to make them feel they are of use," she said. The young women formed "Act" in late September.

> "We have many dreams, including having a women's drama group," said Mousa. The group plans first to coach young talented women, who want to act but do not know how to start.

> She said that the first step is to invite a women's drama group from the Eastern Province to perform in Riyadh. "By doing this we want to send a message to the young women of Riyadh that it's okay to act. Girls here are somehow hesitant due to the strict social environment. Seeing other women of their age acting would encourage them," Mousa said.

In the realm of puppetry, the Dramatic Arts Center of Iran organizes the International Puppet Theatre Festival. It is held biennially in September in Tehran. The program includes Iranian and foreign performances, workshops and research presentations, and street performances. Elsewhere in the MENA one finds, for example, the Cairo

Puppet Theatre, Lebanese Puppet Theatre (Beirut), and the Amazigh Theater Festival in Casablanca, which is centered on the Berbers and their language, and includes both mime and puppetry.

The *hakawātī* (storyteller), who sometimes appears as part of a larger dramatic work, is as a soloist a dying breed in the contemporary MENA. Arabic Literature (in English) (2010), a website, describes Damascene Rashid al-Hallak as one of the few *hakawātīs* left in the Arabic-speaking world. Traditionally they presented their art in cafes. And, though al-Hallak apparently still holds his own against the Ramadan soap operas, there are fears that he may be the last remaining cafe storyteller in Syria. Today, the profession pays poorly. The tips al-Hallak receives each night at the Al-Nawfara cafe amount to around 120 dollars (660LE) a month, far too little to support a family. Notwithstanding this scenario, one of the commentators on the Arabic Literature site has observed a trend in Cairo toward preserving and reviving storytelling in Egypt. Abeer Soliman is a prime mover behind this development, in which she is helped by, among others, El-Warsha. The latter, known for being the first independent troupe in Egypt's free theater movement, is also trying to resuscitate shadow theater, another traditional dramatic form in the MENA. Feeney (1999) describes the fourteenth-century shadow play in Cairo:

> Long or short, simple or elaborate, serious or farcical, the plays were performed in palaces and mud-brick homes alike on such celebratory occasions as weddings and circumcisions—and especially on the nights of the holy month of Ramadan, when Cairenes roused themselves from the day-long fast. Seen in the dark night of a city without neon signs, the dimly illuminated, artfully colored, often hilariously expressive figures with no apparent substance held audiences spellbound.

Amateur and professional theater and puppetry constitute an active part of the modern MENA cultural scene, which is flavored with some typical ingredients of the region. As evidence, consider the following example:

> Dr. Abdul Aziz Bin Mohieddin Khoja, Minister of Culture and Information, inaugurated a five-day festival Sunday at King Fahd Culture Center (KFCC) in Riyadh to mark Universal Children's Day.
>
> In his inaugural speech, the minister stressed the significance of raising children based on Islamic values and Arab culture.

85

A number of officials and other invited dignitaries and guests attended the opening ceremony, along with children from Saudi and international schools.

The Ministry of Culture and Information has licensed a television channel that is operating with content of interest to children, Khoja said referring to Ajyal TV Channel for children.

"My ministry has directly or indirectly engaged in serving the interests of children," he added.

The minister said that organizing events such as children's festivals reflected the Kingdoms policy of taking the utmost care of children and demonstrated King Abdullah's directives in this regard.

The minister took a tour of the exhibition running on the sidelines of the festival and later attended stage performances presented by schoolchildren in the KFCC theaters.

A number of publishing houses, writers and journalists are participating in the event, and as part of cultural activities at the festival, schoolchildren will present dramas, stage and puppet shows. (*Saudi Gazette* 2010)

Oriental Rugs

We left off in chapter 3 with the observation that over the past century the Oriental rug has gained status as a work of art. Today in the West, the appeal of the Oriental rug remains substantial, while in the MENA its economic situation is precarious. This is especially true for Iran, the producer of by far the largest number. The BBC reports that carpet production is now largely mechanized.[20] Nevertheless, traditional hand woven carpets are still made in many parts of the world. They tend to fetch higher prices, in part because they are considered works of art. Modern Iran is the industry leader in both hand- and machine-made carpets.

The handmade carpets are largely the work of women and sometimes children, for such delicate craftsmanship calls for small fingers. Moreover, carpet handicraft is rural, usually located relatively near to the sources of wool and silk where there is also sufficient space to set up a loom and other bulky equipment. The market for these productions, however, is in the big cities in Iran and abroad in the West. The craft is meticulous (e.g., one hundred knots per square inch in a good carpet) and poorly paid, but for all that, a kind of occupational devotion exists. The only amateur makers of the artistic carpets may well be those children who are in the process of learning the distaff family trade.

Architecture

As mentioned in chapter 3, until the middle of the twentieth century, the profession of architecture in Egypt had largely been controlled by foreigners of diverse nationalities (Faculty of Engineering of Cairo University 2011). Following the establishment of schools of engineering, the construction occupations came to be based on engineering education and building knowledge, thus moving from craft to science. In line with this trend, the regulations issued by the Egyptian Syndicate of Engineers shifted the responsibility of building away from national or foreign craftsmen to graduates of these engineering schools.

In Beirut the Faculty of Engineering and Architecture at the American University of Beirut offers architectural training in Lebanon. There is also a school of architecture at the Lebanese American University (formerly Beirut University College), a Faculty of Architecture at Damascus University, the Ecole Supérieure d'Architecture de Casablanca, and so on for the major cities of the MENA. In short, architecture is available for some Arabs and Persians as a serious pursuit, at first as a student-amateur passion then later as a devotee occupation.

Science

It is clear from the websites of the main universities that access to science as a serious pursuit is organized much the same way in the MENA as architecture is, namely by teaching faculties or schools. But is there also, as in the West, a purely amateur science scene, as found primarily in amateur botany, entomology, astronomy, history, mineralogy, ornithology, and archaeology? In the West these pursuits are organized in clubs, associations, and societies, while a number of non-organized scientists operate independently of them (Davidson and Stebbins 2011). Liberal arts hobbyists with a scientific bent also pursue their interests in part by joining these organizations.

The answer to the question is mixed: Astronomy can be studied at the Egyptian Astronomy Club in Cairo, the Dubai Astronomy Group, and the Jordanian Astronomical Society. In ornithology, take note of Birding in Egypt, the Ornithological Society of the Middle East, Birds Oman, Birding in Jordan, Bahrain Bird Report, and Birding in Kuwait, to mention a few. Here is evidence of strong scientific and hobbyist (liberal arts) participation.

By contrast, amateur archaeology, though intensely pursued by some through university courses and tourist expeditions from outside the MENA, is weak at the organizational level. That is, I could find no clubs or associations in the MENA exclusively devoted to this science, although archaeology organizations dot the leisure landscape of Western countries. If nonstudent, amateur archaeology is seldom taken up as a science in the Arab world, there still appears to be a liberal arts hobbyist interest in it. This interest is expressed in some areas of the region as part of a broader fascination with natural history, exemplified in the Qatar Natural History Group (QNHG).

Founded in November 1978 to "bring together people with an interest in the natural history of Qatar and the Gulf,"[21] according to its website, QNHG's interests cover not only all aspects of natural history but also the culture, history, and archaeology of Qatar. Talks are sometimes given as well, on other places of interest to members. Meetings take place between October and June, usually on the first Wednesday of the month. An illustrated talk follows the announcements, and there is a small lending library of books available to members. There are field trips, or "rambles," at least twice a month on Friday or Saturday morning during the season (from mid-October to late April) to places of interest around Qatar. The trips are usually led by people having some knowledge of a particular region or subject, for example, amateur or professional geologists, botanists, and archaeologists. These activities vary in length from a couple of hours walk to a full day excursion. Camping trips and stargazing expeditions are also offered from time to time. Children are welcome on these excursions, but must always be kept under parental control. A number of specialized subgroups have emerged within the main organization.

Elsewhere in the MENA, one finds the Emirates Natural History Group (includes northern Oman), the Bahrain Natural History Society, and the Dubai Natural History Group. Organizations of this nature appear to be mainly hobbyist, offering liberal arts pursuits in the areas of archaeology, botany, entomology, zoology, mineralogy, and ornithology. So, participants specialize in one or a few of these areas, while others take a broader, Renaissance-man approach to natural history in general.

Amateur and hobbyist interest in history in the MENA, if organized manifestations of it are any indication, is also slight. That is, I could only find the Iran Society. It acts as a gathering point for those interested in Iran's heritage and culture, and it claims to be strictly nonpolitical. Its object is to promote learning and advance education about Iran, its peoples and culture, and in particular, to advance education through the study of the language, literature, art, history, religions, antiquities, usages, institutions, and customs of the country.[22]

Sports and Games

Note first that, among the traditional sports discussed in chapter 3, soccer, backgammon, wrestling, weight lifting, and camel racing also form part of the MENA's repertoire of contemporary sports and games. To add to this list, in this section we will look at Arab and Persian participation in world and regional sportive games, particularly as these revolve around the Olympics.

Ray Hanania (2008), starting in 1896 with the advent of the modern Olympic Games, has compiled a summary of Arab participation in those Olympics held in summer. Over the years Egypt, compared with the other MENA countries, has fielded the most participants, in the largest array of events, over the greatest number of years. Using these three criteria Iran (not included in Hanania's analysis) is a close second. The large majority of Arab countries have participated only sporadically, however, typically sending over the years a total of between five to ten athletes to the Olympics. According to Altius Directory's page on the "Summer Olympics," fencing and soccer have drawn teams and individuals from the greatest number of Arab countries (six for each sport), followed by wrestling and weight lifting (four for each sport).[23]

To participate in the world Olympic Games, athletes must be nominated by their national Olympic committee, a decision based on level of performance achieved at one of the world's regional competitions. Every country in the MENA has such a committee. So, to gain a more profound sense of the place of these summer sports in Arab society, we must look at both the Pan Arab Games and the Special Olympics that have been held in the region. The eleventh Pan Arab Games took place in Egypt in 2007. Egypt also hosted the first of these Games in 1953, which have since followed a two-to-four-year schedule in various other countries. Not long after, the seventh Arab Special Olympics regional games took place in the fall of 2010 in Damascus. This was part of a world-wide program, where every two years since 1968, athletes from more than one hundred nations gather at a regional center to celebrate sport and showcase the physical talents of people with intellectual disabilities.

In the MENA, these Olympic Games and Special Olympics consist of only a sample of what the national training programs offer. Although they vary across the region in number and kind of sports offered, many of them include athletics, soccer, bocce, basketball, softball, floor hockey, aquatics, badminton, table tennis, handball, tennis, power lifting, golf, cycling, sailing, judo, gymnastics, and roller skating. A few programs even offer training in winter sports, among them, speed skating, snowshoeing, and snowboarding. Some programs also train rugby and cricket players in two sports that came to the MENA during British occupation.

Why all this talk about elite sports (those pursued by the best athletes in a country) when we are trying to describe the overall level of leisure and community involvement, which is for the most part that of more ordinary people? The answer is that when a country can produce high-level performance in a sport, an exceptional level of local involvement exists in it in one of two ways (Stebbins 2010b). Indeed the internationally visible tip of the sport in question is only possible because of the huge iceberg like base it has in the everyday leisure life of the country. In other words, that involvement may be as spectators of the activity pursued at an amateur or professional level or as amateur or hobbyist participants in the activity. At the professional end of the scale, the spectators usually help pay the wages of the professionals whose games they watch live or on television. Somewhat lower down the scale of excellence among the elite amateurs and hobbyists, spectators support these activities by purchasing tickets from the organizations (e.g., universities, schools, clubs) for which these athletes play. Still farther down, we find the friends and relatives who come to the games of children and adolescents. They typically pay nothing for the opportunity to view these contests. Thus the professionals and elite amateurs and hobbyists have, for the most part, come up through the leisure ranks in their own country. The exceptions to this rule are, in general, the comparatively small numbers of professionals hired from abroad or foreign elite amateurs at institutions of higher education supported by scholarships. Another exception is evident in those totalitarian countries where children are recruited—forcibly if necessary—to become elite amateur athletes, training them exclusively toward excellence in their sport (e.g., the former Soviet Union).

In general there are more spectators than participants, although the ratio is closest to one: one at the child level of participation. As play gets more skilled and players grow older, the best of them get selected to join a decreasing number of teams. At same time more advanced play attracts more spectators. Still love for the sport continues from adolescence on both formally and informally, as teenagers and adults of various ages meet with friends for pickup matches or join clubs or leagues commensurate with their ability. In short, a national sport, even if the rest of the world knows rather little about the degree of passion for it in that country, is pursued enthusiastically in a multitude of ways. Furthermore, notwithstanding male dominance in sport historically in many societies, a national sport seems destined to admit females to the extent they want to participate in it. The modern presence of men's and women's competitions in the various Olympic Games attests to this trend.

The Politics of Sport

Sport in the contemporary MENA is a focal point, perhaps *the* focal point, of tensions in the region spawned by a widespread yearning for European-style modernity. Why? Sport is highly visible (e.g., it is hard to conduct a private football game composed of elite players), a source of national prestige when major victories are scored, and a huge attraction for casual leisure spectators that generates millions of dollars. Moreover, the modern stage of elite sport is global, where all participating nations are exposed to international scrutiny and evaluation of their athletic excellence and how they foster it. What better place, then, for people wanting to subvert state dominance and lay bare instances of corporate weakness to pursue their change-oriented goals while the world looks on? What better place to undermine fissiparousness and oppositionalism than by picking the best athletes to represent the country, rather than by restricting such selection to, for example, tribal or ethnic origins?

It should come as no surprise, given the historical background set out here, that the reactions of the dominant regimes in the MENA to this scenario have usually been conservative, repressive, and sometimes brutal. Let us consider five theaters of political tension that have sprung up in this regard.

One theater is that of female participation in sport in the MENA at all levels, elite and nonelite. Their participation here goes against the grain of traditional culture and the sentiments of the powers that be, though possibly not against the teachings of the Qur'an. Gertrud Pfister (2009), professor at the University of Copenhagen, holds that participation in sport by Muslin females is increasing, even while, "in

91

Islamic countries, women's (and men's) lives and roles are influenced, to a high degree, by the Qur'an and the Hadith, the sayings of the Prophet Muhammad. However, these texts can be read and understood in various ways, and their interpretations are often controversial and contested."

A second theater is that of governmental interference with international sports organizations, which have been established as democratic entities subject only to internal controls and the relevant laws of the country in which they are incorporated. For example, Kirsten Sparre (2006) reported that Iran played poorly at the 2006 World Cup in football. The response of the national government was to fire immediately the president of Iran's football federation and its board of directors, replacing the former with a new president. Although the Fédération Internationale de Football (FIFA) responded by barring Iran from international competition, the President of Iran, Mahmoud Ahmadinejad, refused to change his mind, arguing that his government has the right to change the composition of its football federation. Several coaches and high-profile managers were also released. In a similar action during the same year, Algeria's Minister of Sport dissolved his country's athletics federation, which prompted the International Association of Athletics Federations (IAAF) to ban Algerian athletes from international competitions (Andersen 2006). See Menary (2009) for another such confrontation—also concerning football—although this time in Iraq.

In the third theater we find governmental interference centered on the nationality of competitors in world games, most notably Israel. Frida Ghitis (2008) reported that Iran would not allow one of its swimmers to compete against an Israeli in the 2008 Summer Olympics in Beijing. Something similar happened in judo in the 2004 Olympics in Greece, when an Iranian athlete disqualified himself rather than fight an Israeli for the gold. The former was said to have had an excellent chance to win the title.

Then there is the theater of apparel. Women, having finally gained the right to participate in sport in the MENA, still face challenges over what they may wear during competition. Thomas Erdbrink (2011) wrote that:

> not participating in the 2012 London Olympics is a nightmare for every serious athlete, but for the Iranian women's soccer team the defeat was extra bitter after they were disqualified right before a

crucial qualifying match because they wore Islamic headscarves. . . . The officials decided just before the kickoff that the tight headscarves the Iranian players were wearing to cover their hair broke the association's dress code. . . . After Jordan was awarded a 3–0 victory, Iran's players took to the field crying, Press TV, Iranian state TV's English-language outlet, reported.

FIFA officials defended the ban on the headscarf covering a woman's neck as a necessary safety measure. The result: FIFA on July 5, 2012, lifted the ban.

Still another theater is that of brutality or threat thereof toward renowned national athletes, as they are seen by the dominant regime to fan the flames of the Arab Spring. Here we turn to Bahrain for an example, as supplied by Christer Ahi (2011). The government of this country has begun to crack down on "categories of people whose well-known faces and popularity among the crowds would have created a bad image for the rulers." The beating, persecuting, and jailing of recognized athletes are presently common practices in Bahrain, and this merely because they have voiced their antiestablishment opinions in public.

Non-Sportive Games

Games played with decks of cards are hugely popular and varied the world over. Whereas there are a number of different card games played in the Arab MENA, only two seem popular in several of the constituent countries. Thus, according to the website National and Regional Games, the card game called Trex (also known as Trix or Ticks) is popular in many Middle Eastern countries,[24] including Jordan, Kuwait, Lebanon, Palestine, Saudi Arabia, Syria, and United Arab Emirates. Trex is played by four people using a standard international fifty-two-card pack without jokers. Since some skill and experience is needed to play the game well, this game constitutes a present-day serious leisure activity.

"Basra" is a Middle Eastern fishing game, somewhat similar to the Western game of Casino. The National and Regional Games site mentioned above states that "in fishing games each player has a hand of cards and there is a layout of face up cards on the table. Each player in turn plays a card. If it matches a card or cards in the layout, the played card and the matched cards are captured and placed face down in front of the player. If the card played does not match it is added to the layout." This game of chance is, in the language of the SLP, casual leisure of the active entertainment variety. It is played with two to four people using the standard fifty-two-card deck.

Finally, backgammon, dominoes, and chess continue to be popular in the modern MENA. All three lend themselves well to coffee house life, to sociable conversation, drinking tea, and smoking a hookah. Nevertheless, all three constitute serious leisure, in that chess is purely a skilled pursuit, whereas backgammon and dominoes are games of mixed skill and chance.

Gambling

Being an activity that contravenes the Qur'an, gambling among Muslim Arabs is considered deviant. The World Casino Directory (2011) lists casinos only in Egypt, Lebanon, Morocco, and the United Arab Emirates (UAE), which are nevertheless legally established. Still, these places are, presumably, tourist attractions, thus serving the leisure interests of non-Muslim visitors from outside the region. But the World Casino Directory assures that, "if one looks really hard, you will find places to gamble in the Middle East." The website has a search to aid viewers in their quest. Poker, apart from its international availability online, may be legally played face-to-face in the MENA only in the Casino du Liban situated outside Beirut.

The World Casino Directory holds that horse racing and pari-mutuel facilities are far more popular than casinos in this region. It says that "horse racing in Dubai has become the best in the world with major events also held in Bahrain, Abu Dhabi, Saudi Arabia and even Iraq [especially in Baghdad]. With a purse of US$6 million to the winner, March 2009 saw the 14th running of the richest horse race in the world, the Dubai World Cup." As above, we have no idea how much of the patronage of these events comes from Muslim Arabs. Only Algeria, Egypt, and Syria have state-run lotteries.

Other Amateur and Hobbyist Leisure

Sport and games (other than those of chance) make up only part of the total repertoire of serious leisure activities. This section centers on the nature and extent of these kinds of leisure. This is an imprecise undertaking, in that the sources available for identifying amateur and hobbyist leisure are not designed to cover all manifestations of it in any given community.

It is evident, according to my Internet sample of cities and countries, that governments in the MENA offer instruction in a variety of hobbies and amateur activities in art, sport, and entertainment. They also sponsor festivals, expositions, concerts, shows, and the like in some of these. Municipal and national governments often give operating grants to sports clubs and programs nurturing interest and excellence in a particular activity. The following urban governments were examined using these URLs. They give an aperçu of sport, leisure, and recreational activities there:

Amman: http://www.absoluteastronomy.com/topics/amman

Baghdad: http://www.absoluteastronomy.com/topics/baghdad

Beirut: http://www.absoluteastronomy.com/topics/beirut

Cairo: http://www.encyclopedia.com/topic/cairo.aspx#1-1G2:3426000016-

Damascus: http://www.absoluteastronomy.com/topics/damascus

Dubai: http://www.absoluteastronomy.com/topics/dubai

Tehran: http://www.absoluteastronomy.com/topics/tehran

Tunis: http://www.absoluteastronomy.com/topics/tunis

Capital cities in other Arab MENA countries are not listed here because an absoluteastronomy.com page or equivalent for them cannot be found; the page exists but contains little or no information on sport, leisure, and recreation; or the page has been withdrawn.

A somewhat more precise way to gain an understanding of the leisure scene of a city in the MENA is to explore its Yellow Pages using the online service of www.wayp.com. (Under the header Select Continent, choose Africa for the Maghreb or Asia for the other MENA countries.) After examining the listings on these pages for the eight cities listed in the preceding paragraph, as well as the websites listed there, I was able to reach the following conclusion. *There is in these places sufficient support for amateurs in art, sport, and entertainment and for people who would like to experiment with, if not start, a leisure career in one of them.* By support I mean presence of an effective, relevant, local social world, including availability of instruction, equipment, places to engage in the activity, and by inference, groups or networks of like-minded enthusiasts. By sufficient I mean that a reasonable range of hobbies and amateur activities has been uncovered through these websites. The full range, however, if it can be found anywhere in the world, is certainly not available in the MENA. (I found no mention of entertainment magicians or stand-up comics, for example, or [see below] amateur scientific pursuits on these sites.)

What about amateur science? I could find no mention of clubs or organizations devoted to, say, astronomy, history, entomology, or archaeology. Still, we saw earlier that science is important in the contemporary MENA, suggesting that leisure interests in it are also being pursued. One way this is done is, as already noted, through the amateur role of student. Furthermore, at universities and high schools, in addition to courses and laboratories, there may be clubs for students in, say, astronomy or history. And there may well be clubs outside these institutions that are just not publically accessible in their name by a telephone number or website.

Two Special Hobbies

Two hobbies deserve special mention: the first of which is falconry, a traditional pastime that survives to this day. Commonly referred to as a sport, it is most accurately conceptualized in the SLP as a hobby. That is, it is not usually based on interhuman competition as true sport is. (For his definition of sport, see Coakley [2001, 20].) The other is the liberal arts hobby of reading, which always offers the possibility of acquiring rebellious thoughts that might be turned into rebellious actions.

Falconry (hunting with any trained raptor) continues as a hobby in the MENA, though these days, framed by governmental protective regulations. Roger Upton (2010) sets out the history of falconry in the region, noting its continued popularity today. And this holds despite urbanization and the relentless conversion of wild lands to farming and industrial development. The UAE, arguably the leading Arab country in this hobby, has several clubs, including its most famous: the UAE Falconers' Club. Its mission is evident in the following quotation: "Falconry . . . one of the precious gifts passed on to us from our ancestors' legacy. . . . The sport that lets our children experience the magic of the desert and instills in them the virtue of patience, strong will and a team spirit. . . . Conservation of the Houbara is a necessity to the preservation of the heritage of falconry while we are progressing in modern life."[25] Besides the hunters—the falconers themselves—there are also hobbyist breeders and entertaining competitions where the public can view the skills of these birds.

Turning to the reading of books, of which Middle Easterners are reputed to do little (*The Economist* 2012), book clubs and similar social gatherings centered on reading nevertheless exist. One vibrant example is the Diwan Bookstore in Cairo (see http://www.diwanegypt.com). Beyond selling books, music, and movies it offers discussion sessions on particular books and signing events for new releases. There are a handful of bookstores in Beirut, among them Malik's and Dar Bistro and Books, but I could find no online information about any clubs affiliated with them. The Etana Press bookstore in Damascus runs literary clubs for children and adults.[26] Saudi Arabia's literary clubs operate in nearly every city and have become tiny outposts for free expression and women's rights. They seem to have formed independently of the local bookstores, if there are any. Club meetings are attended mostly by small crowds of intellectuals, however, while the government closely monitors their activities (The Media Line Staff 2011). In fact, censorship of books and discussion groups focused on particular works is an omnipresent threat in the MENA. Despite this situation *The Economist* (2012) reports that a number of books about the Arab Spring have been published (some written in rhyme), which cut a big figure at the Cairo book fair in January 2012.

This attention to literary outlets in the MENA can also be taken as a measure of the level of hobbyist interest in the liberal arts pastimes. The preceding list suggests these outlets are thin in this region. But a word of caution: there may be more, possibly many more, bookstores and affiliated community activities whose online presence is only presented in Arabic, a language I regret being unable to read. By the way, bookshops in hotels, airports, and similar establishments were not examined, primarily because they are small and serve a transient clientele many of whom are not Muslim Arabs.

Community Involvement

First, note that, in keeping with our theoretic discussion in chapter 1 of community involvement, that all collective kinds of amateur and hobbyist activity may also be classified as such. The object of the present section is to go beyond this area of involvement to examine that achieved through volunteering, the third type of serious leisure. We'll also look briefly at project-based volunteering. Casual leisure volunteering will therefore not be systematically covered here.

Let us start with the broadest generalization that I can make that bears on community involvement in the MENA: such involvement is possible there through participation in a fair range of activities. They include volunteer work with youth, women, the elderly, religious groups, and charitable organizations devoted to particular causes (e.g., care, disabilities, sport, education, leisure activities, environmental issues). Museums and zoos also engage volunteers. The adjective "nonprofit" appears infrequently in the online literature centered on community involvement in the MENA, but the organizations using volunteers would be described as such were they located in the West. As evidence for this community involvement, I used again www.wayp.com to explore the Yellow Pages. Six countries' Yellow Pages were amenable to this approach: Tunisia, Oman, Libya, Egypt, Morocco, and Lebanon. (The Yellow Pages in the other countries, if they have them, are business-to-business compendia.) Cairo's Yellow Pages offer the best example, listing hundreds of charitable, nonprofit, social service, and development organizations.[27] Volunteer outlets of the sort just mentioned can be found here. Casablanca appears unique in the region, for it seems to be the only city with a volunteer center: l'Association des oeuvres bienfaisance (bénévoles). Nonetheless, a similar organization called the Charity Vault exists in Tehran.[28] But again, if there are Yellow Pages in Arabic, I would have missed those.

Another indicator is the presence in MENA cities of local Rotary International clubs. According to the Rotary website, "there's something that all Rotary club members have in common: We take action. As community volunteers, we reach out to neighbors in need. We build, support, and organize. We save lives. We work locally and globally."[29] To the extent that members honor this commitment, Rotarian volunteering occurs in Casablanca, Algiers, Cairo, Beirut, Amman, and Dubai, which are the six cities in the MENA with one or more local clubs.

In addition there are some broader signs of community involvement and opportunities for volunteering in such activity. A main one is the Association for Volunteer Services (AVS) located in Lebanon.[30] It describes itself as a nonprofit, nonsectarian, nongovernmental organization, which was legally registered in October 1999. According to its website:

> AVS serves as a national volunteer center—working with, and in support of, its affiliated agencies (nongovernmental organizations, social service institutions, educational institutions, municipalities, government ministries, and businesses committed to corporate volunteering). Its objectives are: to promote, facilitate and improve volunteering and community service throughout Lebanon, to

empower individuals with the realization that they can (and should) make a positive difference in their society through volunteering, and to bridge social barriers through encouraging the different sectors of society to work together for the good of all.

The strategy of AVS is not to stop at the borders of Lebanon, but rather "to promote, facilitate, and improve volunteering and community service throughout Lebanon and beyond." It has been developing programs and providing consultation and training on all aspects of volunteerism, not only in Lebanon but also in Egypt, Kuwait, the UAE, and Syria. For the period 2009–2012, AVS is for the Arab Nations their regional representative to the International Association for Volunteer Effort (IAVE). Additionally, AVS has, since 2003, been Lebanon's National Representative to IAVE.

Much more recently the Arab Thought Foundation (ATF) has launched "The Arab Initiative to Foster a Culture of Volunteering." Designed to coincide with the International Year of Volunteers +10 in 2011, the ATF hoped to galvanize individuals, organizations, service institutions, schools, universities, governmental agencies, and socially responsible businesses throughout the Arab World to work together to strengthen and improve volunteering in the region.[31] Two of the goals of ATF are especially germane to the scope of this book:

> 3. Provide basic training, as well as orientation to other training opportunities available, with the goal of expanding and improving the core of specialists in volunteerism in the Arab World, drawing on Arab cultural traditions and experiences, as well as expertise from within the region and worldwide....
>
> 5. Encourage setting positive national policies for volunteers and volunteerism in the region, through providing information (samples and support).

In sum, opportunities for volunteering abound in the MENA. But, according to estimates of the level of this kind of community involvement made by Arabs themselves, there remains considerable room for improvement. Moreover, official opposition exists, as exemplified in the attempted crackdown on nonprofits promoting democracy and human rights by Egypt's military rulers (Myers and Kirkpatrick, 2011). Notable corporate weakness is still apparent.

Both serious, career volunteering and project-based, noncareer volunteering are implied in this section. For example, Shirin spends three hours each week instructing visitors at the local zoo, a career volunteer post she has held for four years. By contrast, Mohammed has time and interest for only a one-shot volunteer project, in his case, helping organize the publicity for a music festival to be held in his town. In both examples, casual leisure volunteers will also be needed, for example someone to give directions to the exhibits at the zoo and someone to take tickets at the gate to the music festival.

Casual Leisure

Whereas this book is primarily about serious and project-based leisure in the MENA, casual leisure, as just exemplified, does have a role to play in cultural development. This is evident in a person's search for an OLL. The term refers to the deeply rewarding and interesting pursuit during free time of one or more substantial, absorbing forms of serious leisure, complemented by judicious amounts of casual leisure or project-based leisure, if not both. People find their OLL by partaking of leisure activities that individually and in combination enable them to realize their human potential, leading thereby to self-fulfillment and enhanced well-being and quality of life (Stebbins 2000b).

An OLL rests on finding an appealing balance among the three forms, a point that is sometimes easy to forget in the zealous promotion of serious and project-based leisure. For instance, one of the favorite casual pastimes of many of the people I have interviewed over the years was engaging in what might be called leisure shoptalk: spirited sessions of sociable conversation about their pursuit held with like-minded enthusiasts. More generally, serious leisure typically demands significant energy and concentration, two patently exhaustible resources. If and when exhaustion sets in and some free time remains, one type or another of casual leisure is sure to be sought as a complement. Chances are good, too, that it will be television.

Casual leisure is alive and well in the MENA, the consequences of which have not escaped Djaït's (2011) critical eye. He says that "we [Arabs in the MENA] have been content to borrow the superficial aspect of modernity, but we have adopted nothing fundamental. . . . It is certain that our culture does not prepare us for a refined conception of happiness, extreme and strong . . . but it prepares us rather for apathetic modes of happiness while those who are more favored wear themselves out by seeking excessive pleasures and expressing themselves in ostentation" (xxiv). In Iran a study using a random sample of women living in Shiraz found that they were primarily interested in home-based activities, including most commonly, TV and radio, family gatherings, and reading (Arab-Moqhaddam, Henderson, and Sheikholeslami 2007). The least participation occurred in the cultural, scientific (i.e., profession based), and artistic activities.

Today many Arabs have access to local, regional, and international entertainment television. Al-Bab, whose goal is to introduce non-Arabs to the Arabs and their culture, describes the contemporary situation in television in the MENA.[32] In so doing, the service explains why TV is so popular there. The authors of this site observe that, until the 1990s, nearly every television channel was governmentally owned and rigidly controlled. These channels still operate, but since then, satellite television has appeared, bringing with it some significant changes. Privately owned, nongovernmental channels have "introduced livelier programmes aimed at a pan-Arab audience and also adopted a more professional approach to news and current affairs." The news channel, al-Jazeera, is considered a pioneer in this area which, though financed by the government of Qatar, enjoys considerable independence. Al-Jazeera, many of whose staff originally came from the BBC, became the first Arabic channel to provide extensive live news coverage. The service even sent reporters to previously unthinkable places, such as Israel. Al-Jazeera also broke new ground with its discussion programs, looking at issues from more than one angle and often raising subjects previously tabooed.

Al-bab.com reports that in 2008, at a meeting called by Egypt and Saudi Arabia, Arab information ministers approved, in an attempt at state dominance, a charter to regulate satellite broadcasting. This, says Al-Bab, was widely viewed as an attempt to control this medium. See this same Internet page for a list of news and general television channels in the MENA. Also on this page is a lengthy discussion of the popularity of the Internet and governmental attempts to control its use as well.

Turning to other kinds of casual leisure, we saw in chapter 3 that many an Arab spends some time in the cafes and hookah (water pipe) bars as well as in the suqs. In these establishments relaxation and sociable conversation are dominant attractions. Most countries in the MENA have beaches, where people may swim, suntan, and engage in other outdoor casual leisure activities. Annual film festivals take place in several countries, featuring both Arab and foreign films. Listening to Arabic poetry and music continues to be popular. Additionally, though as just noted, outlets for stand-up comedy are not to be found in the Yellow Pages, this dramatic art *is* practiced in the

MENA, exemplified in the annual Amman Stand-Up Comedy Festival (founded in 2008) and Yemen's first comedy show offered in 2010 (*The Economist* 2011b). There are few jokes about Islam, but fellow citizens and the government get routinely and roundly lampooned. Finally, we looked earlier at the games of chance as a variety of active entertainment and the spectator sports as popular passive entertainment. The second joins television and casual reading to lengthen the list of inactive diversions.

Conclusion

Compared with what could be said on the subject, this has been a brief and incomplete survey of contemporary leisure and community involvement in the MENA. Still, it should be adequate as a picture of leisure in the modern Muslim Arab/Iranian world, giving detail sufficient to serve as a foundation for discussing leisure's role in cultural development there. It was pointed out in chapter1 that every known society has leisure, even though it may not be recognized by this concept when talked about in the local language. Every society recognizes time away from obligation, be it work or nonwork obligatory activity. The present chapter has amply demonstrated the presence of leisure in the MENA.

Even the three cultural obstacles have by no means fully inhibited it. The seemingly unyielding tribal oppositionalism, omnipresent corporate weakness, and weight of state dominance have certainly combined to weaken the pursuit of some kinds of serious leisure and community involvement, not to mention participation in certain types of casual and project-based leisure. But cultural development in free time is still possible in the MENA.

Notes

18. Source: http://icon-ik.com/wordpress/?p=767, retrieved 28 August 2011.
19. Source: http://orfali.net; http://www.daralanda.com, retrieved 29 August 2011.
20. Source: http://www.bbc.co.uk/persian/business/story/2007/07/070701_ka-carpet-iranian.shtml, retrieved 23 February 2012.
21. Source: http://www.qnhg.org, retrieved 26 July 2011.
22. Source: http://www.iransociety.org, retrieved 26 July 2011.
23. Source: http://www.altiusdirectory.com/Sports/summer-olympics.php, retrieved 23 February 2012.
24. Source: http://www.pagat.com/national, retrieved 10 August 2011.
25. Source: http://www.emiratesfalconersclub.com, retrieved 11 August 2011.
26. See http://www.thara-sy.com/TharaEnglish/modules/news/article.php?storyid=230, retrieved 13 August 2011.

27. See http://www.yellowpages.com.eg/category/charitable,-non_profit-and-social-services-and-development-organizations/ODI1X19fIF9fX18gXw==, retrieved 13 August 2011.
28. Source: http://charity-charities.org/Iran-charities/Tehran.html, retrieved 16 August 2011.
29. Source: http://www.rotary.org/en/Pages/ridefault.aspx, retrieved 16 August 2011.
30. See http://www.avs.org.lb/main.html, retrieved 16 August 2011.
31. Source: http://www.arabthought.org/en/node/376, retrieved 16 August 2001.
32. Source: http://www.al-bab.com/media/television.htm, retrieved 16 August 2011.

5

Leisure, Work, and Cultural Development

Hichem Djaït (2011, 136) has written a powerful justification for this chapter. He states:

> it is obvious that the outside world must help the Arabs to break free of their isolation, and of the incomprehension in which they suffocate; to incorporate them into humanity in such a way that the Arab world will be at peace, and will be truly accepted among the community of nations. It is clear that the Arabs themselves must also advance in this direction: that of détente, of peace, of democracy, and human rights. (136)

Another justification has been expressed by Thomas Friedman (2011) who was writing about the Arab Spring:

> As I've tried to argue, this uprising, at root, is not political, it's existential. It's more about Albert Camus than Che Guevara. All these Arab regimes to one degree or another stripped their people of their basic dignity. They deprived them of freedom and never allowed them to develop anywhere near their full potential. And as the world has become hyper-connected, it became obvious to every Arab citizen just how far behind they were—not only to the West, but to China, India and parts of sub-Saharan Africa.

This lack of freedom to develop "anywhere near their full potential" is what we have been referring to in this book as self-fulfillment.

This chapter offers outside help leading to cultural development in the MENA, but strives to do this by working with the kinds of leisure and community involvement described in the preceding chapter. My intention is to show in detail how Arabs and Iranians can develop themselves through such activities, hopefully inspiring them to pursue some of the activities that are religiously, geographically, and financially available to them. Together these can add up to an agreeable lifestyle the main parts of which generate well-being and self-fulfillment. In the language of the field of leisure studies, this chapter is one of leisure education, of educating people in the MENA about the serious pursuits available to them in their free time.

This chapter will, in general, follow the outline of chapter 2. We will spend most of our time looking at the fulfilling serious and project-based activities as well as those falling under the heading of community involvement. In the main, we will look at (1) availability of these activities as framed within religious, cultural, geographic, and financial constraints; (2) finding opportunities to pursue them; and (3) launching and continuing a leisure career in these activities.

Some readers may argue that all this is mission impossible. To quote again professor Djaït (2011):

> We [the Arabs] are in fact more apt to resist than to be creative and to search for happiness or fulfillment. Happiness, for us, means monotony and is limited to the maintenance of social and family ties. If we escape from routine, it is only to display uncontrollable ostentation and excessive spending. (xviii)

My interest is to lay out ways to reduce this resistance, which is negative and problem-oriented, by accentuating the positive (on this point, see also Djaït [2011, xv]) through finding well-being and fulfillment in serious (leisure and work) pursuits. Elsewhere I have argued that leisure as defined in this book is a main foundation of a positive existence (Stebbins 2009b).

My general stance in this chapter, then, is that the resources exist in much of the MENA that can enable its people to develop themselves as individuals. They can do this through free-time activities and thereby find a balanced lifestyle built on, in substantial part, one or more serious pursuits. Accordingly, this is a practical (i.e., educational) chapter, predicated on the assumption that, to find a career in one or a few of these pursuits and to start building this lifestyle, beginners need detailed, down-to-earth information on how to reach these goals.

The Serious Pursuits

In chapter 4 we inventoried many of the contemporary MENA's amateur-professional activities in the arts. Let us now note that, in pursuing any one of them, participants will face certain constraints. This is possibly most evident in literature, theater, and painting, where enthusiasts face significant political and religious constraints, but can also be seen in Oriental rug making in Iran, which is geographically limited to certain rural areas of the country. There are also cultural prohibitions about women acting onstage with men, while the Oriental dance is stigmatized by some as deviant. Moreover, some worry that pop music, being sexually suggestive, grates on the sensibilities of the conservative religious authorities. Arabs and Iranians opting for a fulfilling leisure-work career in these contentious areas will face the risks of state dominance and, to avoid censorious challenges as much as possible, will need a well-crafted defense of their passion. But even that may be insufficient to avoid trouble.

Controversial or not, would-be participants in the artistic pursuits must find opportunities to observe the art of interest, obtain instruction in it, produce it, find a leisure and possibly a work career in it, and so on. The following sections lay out variety of suggestions along these lines. Their content, originally developed for North America (Stebbins 1998), has been adapted as much as possible to the present social, cultural, and economic situation in the MENA as it bears on leisure and devotee work there. As stated in the Introduction the spirit of these suggestions is that of energizing and facilitating self-help in the local MENA community rather than laying down elitist directives from afar.

Music

Bear in mind, in reading the following list, that folk music played by the folk in their local community is best classified as a form of activity participation and is therefore presented later. Its commercial manifestation, in part because it is subject to the demands of the entertainment market and the need to making a living from playing it, tends to stray significantly from its folkloric origins.

Art

> chamber music
> choral singing
> jazz (vocal, instrumental)
> operatic singing
> orchestral music

Commercial

> country music
> folk music (commercial)
> rock music and its many derivatives

Art music demands private lessons, or more rarely class instruction, in voice or on an instrument, constituting thereby the main port of entry into the world of amateur, and later for some, professional music. None of the five forms can be executed at a reasonably satisfying level without a certain amount of formal training. Private lessons are usually available in many of the larger cities of the MENA for voice, the more popular Western instruments (guitar, flute, cello, trumpet, trombone, violin, piano, clarinet, percussion, saxophone), and the principal Middle Eastern instruments. To locate a teacher, look in the Yellow Pages of the telephone directory (use www.wayp.com) under such headings as "Music Colleges" and "Music Teachers." But, since not all music teachers are listed here, ask a musical friend or acquaintance to suggest someone. Established amateurs and professionals typically know a number of vocalists and instrumentalists and can, using these informal connections, put the novice in touch with an effective teacher. Other good sources of information include high school music teachers, college and university departments of music, and the musicians in the community's amateur and professional musical groups. The personnel working at the music stores can usually suggest teachers for the instruments they sell and rent, and they may even give lessons themselves. If there is an equivalent of the musicians unions in the West (although I could find no evidence of this in the MENA), employees at its office may know of some of the music teachers in town. People interested in a jazz or folk-music instrument might seek information on teachers from a local jazz or folk-music club. However a teacher is found, the beginner should indicate the type of music he or she eventually wants to pursue (i.e., jazz, folk, rock, country, orchestral). Once they have imparted the basics of playing the instrument, its teachers tend to specialize in one of these types.

Class instruction is occasionally available on certain instruments, most commonly as part of an adult education program, where students learn mostly by playing in a small band, chamber group, or symphony orchestra. And choral training is by nature collective, consisting of group instruction or personal instruction offered through the chorus or choir. Although adult education courses are sometimes available here, too, most adult amateurs seem to enter choral singing through a church choir, community chorus, or barbershop chorus. College and university students may have, at their institution, access to a chorus, an a cappella group, or an orchestra, although these ensembles may only accept experienced musicians. Finally, these days, question-and-answer services exist on the Internet, such as Yahoo Answers (http://answers.yahoo.com), Answers.com (http://www.answers.com), and Answerbag (http://www.answerbag.com), enabling people who want instruction in any serious leisure activity to ask where to find it.

Beginning instrumentalists buy, rent, or borrow the musical instrument on which they intend to become proficient. It is wise to seek advice on this matter from an experienced musician, preferably a music teacher. Except for those playing the pipe organ or the orchestral percussion instruments, established Western amateurs almost always own their instruments. But beginners anywhere in the world will want to determine their commitment to this kind of serious leisure before making such a purchase, which may be costly.

Dance

The five fine-art forms of amateur/professional dance are jazz, tap, ballet, choral (show), and modern. Although private lessons are also available in the entertainment forms of ballroom and country and western dancing, beginners in the fine-arts forms most commonly get their start in classes. The Yellow Pages (www.wayp.com), under such headings as "Dance Studios" and "Dance Academies," offer possibly the best list of the community's instructional opportunities in this art. Insider advice on which studio to select may be sought from friends and acquaintances who know the local scene for the dance in question or, for jazz, ballet, and modern dance, from the dance department of a nearby college or university. In fact, such departments have their own introductory courses in jazz, ballet, and modern dance, which are usually open to all full- and part-time students attending the college or university. Performing dance troupes, both amateur and professional, also have information on how to enter their kind of dance.

Theater

This class of activities is one of the most varied of the serious artistic pursuits.

Fine Arts

    art cinematic production
    art pantomime
    classical community
    commercial community (musical, operetta, comedy, drama)
    experimental community

Entertainment

> commercial cinematic production (home film and video)
> entertainment magic
> entertainment pantomime
> public speaking
> puppetry
> sketch
> stand-up comedy
> variety arts (juggling, clowning, ventriloquism, acrobatics)

A one or two semester-length drama course is normally all that is needed to learn the basic principles of acting. The same may be said for puppetry. The courses are noncredit when taught in an adult education program, whereas they must be taken for credit when taught at a college or university. In the latter, however, students are often allowed to enroll in the introductory courses even though they are majoring in fields other than drama. Stores selling and renting theatrical costumes, supplies, and equipment (often listed in the Yellow Pages) may be able to steer beginners toward the classes they need. In the final analysis, however, most of the art of drama is learned on the job, by landing a part in a play and then working with the director to interpret it appropriately and imaginatively. As for beginning courses in cinematic production, they are comparatively rare, including in the MENA (using www.wayp.com, I found only one, in Beirut). But such courses may turn up occasionally in the nondegree programs in adult education and regularly in the degree programs in cinematic production offered by a number of community colleges and technical schools.

Beginners in the entertainment dramatic arts other than sketch, puppetry, cinematic production, and commercial community theater acquire their fundamentals in a strikingly different way. This is necessary because formal courses of the kind described for the preceding arts are simply unavailable in most communities in North America and, I am now convinced, in the MENA as well. Thus these beginners must get their start by observing the performances of competent amateurs and professionals and by talking with them about how they learned their art, organize their routines into shows of twenty to forty minutes, and book opportunities to present the shows in public (Stebbins 1984; 1990). Budding entertainment magicians can also receive advice on these questions from established magicians working at the local magician supply stores and from members of one of the local magic clubs (ask at the supply stores about these). New participants in comedy hang around the comedy nightclubs in their community, watching the art in its many expressions, talking with performers and, eventually, presenting their own five-minute spot on amateur night. In both magic and comedy, there is usually a local professional or two who offers individual or group lessons. Inquire at the comedy clubs and magic clubs and supply stores about such instruction and consult the biographical list of Middle Eastern comics on Answers.Com.

Clowning and juggling are learned in much the same way. The local professionals and some of the local amateurs can be contacted directly through their own enterprise or indirectly through an agent (see "Entertainment and Entertainment Bureaus" in the Yellow Pages and look for performers' websites). The personnel at the magic supply stores may know a clown or juggler who gives lessons or at least is willing to talk informally about how to learn their art. In those North American cities where the American Guild of Variety Artists has a local union, office staff may keep a list of such people. I do not know if such organizations exist in the MENA. Finally, for learning about public speaking, note that Toastmasters International has clubs in Egypt, Iraq, Jordan, Kuwait, Lebanon, Oman, Qatar, Saudi Arabia, and the UAE.[33]

Art

Here, too, it is instructive to distinguish fine and commercial art, all of which can be used to interpret such subjects as landscapes, still life, humans, and wildlife.

Fine

drawing (pencil, ink, charcoal)
painting (oils, watercolors)
photography (color, black and white)
print making (relief, intaglio, lithography, serigraphy)
printing (stenciling, lettering, calligraphy)
sculpting (balloons)
sculpting and carving (clay, wood, metal, wire, putty)

Commercial

drawing cartoons, caricatures
painting (oils, watercolors)
photography (color, black and white)
sketching

Beginning amateurs in art can learn the rudiments of painting, drawing, sculpting, printmaking, and photography through the appropriate noncredit courses given in adult education or the appropriate credit courses given by the art schools and the college and university art departments. Alternatively, they may enroll in the beginners' classes offered at some of the local art studios and art supplies stores. To locate these, as noted in the preceding chapter, consult the Yellow Pages in the telephone directories of the larger cities, looking under the heading of "Art Lessons." Art suppliers not themselves in the instruction business can normally be counted on to furnish a decent overview of the local opportunities in art instruction for beginners. Calligraphy lessons are sometimes listed under this heading in the Yellow Pages, although looking for instruction in this art under "art lessons" may be the more fruitful approach. A Yellow Pages in Arabic may contain far more information on calligraphy than the ones in English and French, my zone of linguistic competence.

Commercial instruction in photography—instruction offered by a business establishment—can be obtained at the studios of some of the professional photographers in town. (Look under headings such as "Photography Courses" in the Yellow Pages, but do not expect to find much in the MENA.) Apart from basic instruction in drawing, no formal training exists for would-be cartoonists and caricaturists. Instruction in printing should be sought through the noncredit courses offered in adult education or through the credit courses given in an established graphic design program at a technical school. Instructional manuals in all areas of art are available from the supplies outlets, but be aware that evaluation by an experienced artist of the beginner's painting or photography, for example, is absolutely essential if the latter is to find fulfillment in the activity and enjoy a leisure career there. The instructor usually meets this need for students enrolled in his or her course. Again, it should be understood that manuals serve most effectively as supplements to rather than substitutes for courses and lessons.

Literature

Aspiring writers should search the catalogues of the colleges, universities, and adult education programs for introductory courses on writing fiction, nonfiction, and poetry. Some of the college and university courses may have prerequisites, commonly one or two literature courses, which invariably limit their accessibility to a relatively small number of full- and part-time students. Although there are books for writers, these resources are never fully self-sufficient, for beginners especially need editing and need to have their work criticized by seasoned authors. The teachers of the introductory courses fill this crucial role in the first instance. As for the Yellow Pages, in the MENA as in North America, very little comes up when searching under such headings as "writing lessons," "creative writing," and "writing courses." Terms of this sort seem most likely to put the searcher in touch with programs designed to teach a language, usually Arabic, English, or French.

Sport

The list below distinguishes team and individual sports, those that offer an amateur to professional career, and those that offer a career leading to elite amateur status. The latter refers to sports in the Olympics Games and the world's regional games, where the countries that the athletes represent provide for their livelihood.

Team Sports (professional)

    baseball
    basketball
    cricket
    football (American, Canadian, Australian, etc.)
    football (soccer)
    hockey
    roller hockey
    rugby

Team Sports (elite amateur)

    bobsledding
    field hockey
    rowing
    synchronized swimming
    volleyball
    water polo
    yachting

Individual Sports (professional)

    auto racing
    bowling
    boxing
    equestrian events
    figure skating
    golf
    jai alai (including doubles)
    motorcycle racing

racquetball (including doubles)
rodeo (calf roping, steer wrestling, bull riding, etc.)
squash
tennis (including doubles)

Individual Sports (elite amateur)

alpine skiing and snowboarding
archery
athletics (track and field events)
badminton (including doubles)
canoe and kayak racing
cross-country skiing
cycling
diving
fencing
gymnastics
handball
luge
martial arts
sailing
shooting (firearms)
ski jumping
speed skating
swimming
weight lifting
wrestling (excluding entertainment wrestling)

Generally speaking, the sports are, in many parts of the world, one of the easiest forms of serious leisure to enter, and most of the sports and the ways of entering them are well known. Indeed, many adult amateurs in the collective sports began their athletic careers there as adolescents, and although they may have momentarily reduced their participation at some point in their adult years, they are hardly beginners when they reenter. To a lesser degree, the same can be said for the players of many of the individual sports. For anyone, then, getting started in a sport is problematic.

But, in some team sports, the teams are composed of disproportionate numbers of players who joined the team with no prior experience in the sport; in the MENA, these include yachting, rowing, water polo, and synchronized swimming (the latter two being pursued mostly in Egypt and Iran). Few adults or high school students are likely to get the opportunity to participate in these sports, even if they live in communities where they are routinely played. A beginner living in a community where people yacht or bobsled, for example, faces two problems if this person wants to become involved there: how to contact a team and how to wangle an invitation to join it. Perhaps the most effective way of solving these problems is to hang around the places where people engage in the activity: the wharf, river, bobsled run, or swimming pool. Talk to the participants, asking about the nature of the activity, the ways a person can become involved, and the kinds of qualifications he or she is expected to have. In some communities these sports are organized in clubs, which as long as they can be located, makes access easier. Check the Yellow Pages under such headings as "Clubs" and "Associations" or inquire at a nearby college or university in the unit variously known these days as the faculty (or department) of recreation, leisure studies, kinesiology, or physical education.

Adult beginners in some of the individual sports may get started by taking lessons. This is certainly a common approach for novices in golf, tennis, bowling, swimming, diving, archery, gymnastics, and the equestrian events. Lessons in these sports are sometimes advertised in the Yellow Pages. Alternatively, one can inquire at a golf or tennis club or a municipal swimming pool. Supplies and equipment stores specializing in these sports often maintain a list of instructors, which is where a beginner should seek such information for archery. Instruction in any of these sports as well as in squash, handball, racquetball, badminton, ski jumping, and alpine and cross-country skiing (see chapter 4 for the list of winter sports in the MENA) may also be offered from time to time in small classes given in an adult education program or in an equivalent community-oriented program sponsored by a college or university recreation or kinesiology department. Instruction in alpine skiing is often given on-site at the ski hills. Community sports centers, the Young Men's Christian Association (YMCA), and the Young Women's Christian Association (YWCA) also offer lessons and playing opportunities in a number of these sports. There are YMCAs and YWCAs in Egypt, Jordan, and Lebanon. Classes in target shooting are sometimes available at the firing ranges in the area (see the Yellow Pages under a heading like "Shooting Clubs"). Finally, the Yellow Pages classification of "Horses, Riding, Stables and Equipment" (e.g., Egypt), "Horses" (e.g., Lebanon, Jordan), or their equivalent will help the reader find instruction in the equestrian hobbies.

A few of the individual sports must be approached by a beginner much as he or she would approach the team sports of yachting, rowing, and the like: by hanging around the scene and showing an interest by asking questions. These individual sports include rodeo and auto and motorcycle racing. The remaining sports—judo, boxing, cycling, jai alai, canoe/kayak racing (chiefly in Iran), weight lifting, track and field events—are highly specialized and often organized in clubs (or gyms for weight lifters). A combination of frequenting around the scene and inquiring at the club's office are two fruitful ways to explore entry into these sports. In the Yellow Pages look under "Sporting Clubs" or "Clubs," some of which offer instruction and playing opportunities in one or more of these activities. Equipment stores, particularly those in cycling and canoeing, are useful centers of information about races and the ways to participate in them. It may be possible to take up wrestling only through a college, university, or national team; this limits participation to registered students or invited participants.

Science

My research on serious leisure involvements in science revealed three kinds of participants: observers, armchair participants, and applied scientists (summarized in Stebbins 1992). The observers are amateurs; they directly experience their objects of interest through scientific inquiry. The armchair participants are liberal arts hobbyists who pursue their interests largely, if not wholly, through reading (more about them later). They hold to their approach either because they prefer it to observation or because they lack the time, equipment, opportunity, or physical stamina to go into the field or laboratory. The applied scientists, who are also amateurs, express their knowledge of a branch of science in some practical way. As far as we know, the most active group of applied amateurs is found in computer science. The amateur observers vary much more than their professional counterparts in their level of knowledge and degree of willingness and ability to contribute original data to their science.

Physical Sciences

astronomy
computer science
meteorology
mineralogy
physics

Biological Sciences

botany
entomology
ornithology

Social Sciences

archaeology
history

If amateur science clubs exist in the MENA beyond those in the educational institutions, the (English) Yellow Pages seem to be of little use in locating them. It is the same in North America. One way around this deficiency in both regions is to contact the appropriate department at a college or university, for instance, the departments of geology or geography for mineralogy, department of physics for astronomy, departments of archaeology or anthropology for archaeology, department of history for local history, and department of computer science for amateur computer science. Note that, in large universities, the three biological sciences may be organized either as separate departments or as quasi-autonomous subdivisions of a general department of biology.

In addition, the community's planetarium may know of the local astronomy club, if it does not actually house it. (A Yellow Pages search in English revealed some "Museums" but nothing on "Planetariums.") And the local office of the national weather service may have contact with the meteorology club in the area. Museums specializing in the history of the community and surrounding area may be extensively involved with the local historical and archaeological societies. Natural history museums may have ties with the region's amateur entomological and ornithological clubs, as well as with certain individual members of those clubs whose work enhances their collections. Although they seem to cater chiefly to hobbyists, the shops selling lapidary equipment and supplies may nevertheless maintain up-to-date information about the town's mineralogical club.

Hobbies

The present section follows the sequence of hobbyist activities set out in chapter 2. We begin therefore with collecting and pass from there to making and tinkering; participating in activities; competing in games, sports, and contests; and pursuing the liberal arts hobbies. One general hint for getting started in a hobby is to search for pertinent books and periodicals in the public libraries as well as the larger book stores and magazine outlets in the community. For an Internet supplier for hobbies of wide variety, see Ediforma Auctions.[34] Here buyers bid on hobbyist supplies and collectibles to be received by mail once the purchase is made. Ediforma ships to most countries in the world.

More specific advice pertaining to each type of hobby is presented below. Discussion is preceded by a list of its subtypes, drawn from the author's book on searching for an OLL through serious leisure (Stebbins 1998). The primary reason for presenting these lists is to show the scope of each subtype and therefore the opportunities available in principle to interested participants. In practice, constraints such as cost, religious scruples, local availability, cultural pressures, and personal tastes and aptitude will rule out some of them for some people wherever they live on this planet. Descriptions of these hobbies are available in Stebbins (1998), Stebbins, (2005a), and Davidson and Stebbins (2011).

Collecting

The following subtypes have so far been identified for collecting:

antique books
antique cars
antique clocks and watches
antiques (general)
antique guns
antique toys
art objects (crafts, like figurines and plates)
art objects (musical instruments)
art objects (paintings, sculptures, etc.)
coins, currency, and medals
dolls
models (airplanes, toys, trains, etc.)
natural objects (leaves, fossils, insects, pearls, starfish, seashells, animal trophies, rocks and minerals, etc.)
popular culture (pins, cards, caps, comic books, etc.)
posters and prints
stamps

The first move in acquiring the object in question is obvious in the collection of natural objects. In other kinds of collecting, the collector typically begins by exploring the street shops and online outlets selling stamps, antiques, coins and currency, or paintings and sculptures. Prints and posters are sold in such places as gift and souvenir shops and the picture framing services. Furthermore, collectors soon learn from colleagues in the hobby and perhaps from clerks in the shops about the existence of shows, auctions, and good quality and reliable mail-order services. Those same clerks may also be able to direct the beginner to a local, regional, or national club or association concerned with a particular kind of collecting; in North America these groups are especially likely to emerge around art, guns, toys, stamps, old cars, and coins and currency.

Making and Tinkering

The subtypes of the making and tinkering hobbies are even more numerous than the collecting hobbies:

    beverage crafts (wine, beer, liqueurs, etc.)
    cooking, baking, and candy making
    decorating activities (collage, gilding, mobiles, stencils, dried flowers, decoupage, ikebana, glass etching, etc.)
    do-it-yourself activities (cars, renovations, repairs, etc.)
    interlacing and interlocking activities (stitching, quilting, basketry, weaving, tapestry, rug hooking, crocheting, knitting, etc.)
    knot-making activities (oriental rug making, fly-tying, macramé, etc.)
    leather and textile activities (sewing, felt crafts, textile dying, clothes making, etc.)
    metalworking activities
    miscellaneous crafts (restoring antique furniture, making perfume, making beads and buttons, plasterwork, staining glass, candle making, kite construction, lapidary work, mosaic work, etc.)
    paper crafts (paper sculpture, origami, book binding, papier-mâché, paper airplanes and helicopters, etc.)
    pottery
    raising and breeding indoor plants
    raising and breeding outdoor plants (gardening, landscaping, arboriculture, etc.)
    raising and breeding pets and show animals (fish, snakes, etc.)
    toy models (ships, rocketry, airplanes, etc.)
    toy puppets and dolls
    toys (dollhouse furnishings)
    toys and games (often made of wood)
    woodworking activities (marquetry, furniture, etc.)

As in collecting, getting started in the making and tinkering hobbies is rarely a mystery. Most people who want to learn to cook or make wine or beer would think to buy or borrow a book on the subject or enroll in one or more classes offered either by a municipal adult education program or a related business (e.g., wine shop, kitchen supply store). It is likewise for the decorative activities—the leather and textile crafts, the interlacing and interlocking activities, and some of the miscellaneous crafts, especially candle making and mosaic making—except that the supporting businesses are the local craft shops and online sources. In the same vein, some of the hobby shops and adult education programs may offer the occasional set of classes for budding makers of toys and models. Not to be forgotten are the how-to books, which are available (at least in English) for all the making and tinkering hobbies. In some of these hobbies, notably do-it-yourself activity (often one-shot projects) and wood, metal, and lapidary work, such books may be the main learning resource, since classes seem relatively uncommon everywhere. The public library may carry many of these books. Finally, the social world of each of these hobbies has its commercial equipment and supplies sector (e.g., the craft shop, hardware store, fabric outlet) where advice is readily available from experienced practitioners and pertinent how-to literature (including books) is sold or distributed free of charge.

In this section and the preceding one, the resources have been discussed primarily from a North American perspective. For would-be hobbyists in the MENA, they suggest some possible points of entry to serious or project-based leisure. Since equivalent local resources may not always be available, newcomers to the activity will have to draw on their own ingenuity to find start-up opportunities in their local communities and on the Internet.

Noncompetitive Activity Participation (Artistic)

Activity participants steadfastly pursue a form of leisure requiring systematic physical movement that has intrinsic appeal and is conducted within a set of rules. Often the activity poses a challenge, albeit a noncompetitive one. When carried out continually for these reasons, the activities included in this category are as diverse as fishing, video games, and barbershop singing. Those discussed in this section require some kind of artistry.

> folk art and craft (folk painting, sculpting, ceramics, textiles, etc., as practiced in any culture)
> folk dance, line dances, and Morris dance
> folk music (regional forms, barbershop singing, etc.)
> square dance

Barbershop singing (found mainly in North America, Europe, Australia), square dancing (mainly the United States), and Morris dancing (mainly England) are not, to my knowledge, activities accessible in the MENA. They are listed here only to show the global diversity of this category of activity participation. On the other hand, line dancing, because it is in its multiple forms a genre of folk dance found throughout the world (Powell 2003), may also have its expressions in the MENA. Meanwhile, the MENA is home to a lively indigenous folk-art scene, described in some detail in chapter 4. People wanting to take up an Arab/Iranian type of folk music, theater, or dance are most probably already attending local performances of one or more of these arts. The next step would be for them to ask the performers how to get involved, where to take lessons, and otherwise participate in the performers' social world.

Noncompetitive Activity Participation (Nature Challenge Activities)

A *nature challenge activity* (NCA) is a distinctive type of outdoor pursuit that, in one form or another, appeals to all ages (Davidson and Stebbins 2011). The NCA is leisure whose core activity or activities center on meeting a natural test posed by one or more of six elements: (1) air, (2) water, (3) land, (4) animals (including birds and fish), (5) plants, and (6) ice or snow (sometimes both). A main reason for engaging in a particular NCA is to experience participation in its core activities pursued in a natural setting. In other words, while executing these activities, the special (aesthetic) appeal of the natural environment in which this process occurs simultaneously sets the challenge the participant seeks.

Since the list of NCAs is long, only a sample is presented below. Some of these activities have a competitive side, which attracts some, though not all, of their enthusiasts. (For research on this variation in the appeal of serious leisure activities, see Stebbins [2005a].)

ballooning, flying, and gliding (in a glider)
bird-watching
dirt (trail) bike riding (noncompetitive)
fishing (salt and fresh water)
hang gliding, parasailing
hiking, backpacking, camping
hunting (bow, falconry, firearm)
ice boating
ice skating
mountain climbing
mushroom gathering
parachuting and skydiving
skin (scuba) diving and snorkeling
snowmobiling
snowshoeing
spelunking
surfing
trapping

In North America, adult education courses exist for virtually every participation activity that challenges nature. Beginners interested in such activity should, if it is locally available, head for the Yellow Pages and to the adult education programs operated by their municipal government, nearby colleges and universities, and possibly other providers. Courses in the NCAs may last no more than a day or two or as long as two years or more. For example, it is probable that in the MENA, as in North America, balloonists must be certified, and pilots of planes and gliders must be licensed, both occurring after successfully completing a formal instructional program. Lengthy training is also necessary for parachuting and scuba diving. (See the Yellow Pages, but mostly for scuba, since parachuting is listed only in Cairo.) In fact, a sizeable majority of the North Americans meeting one of nature's challenges as a hobby appear to start out with some kind of formal instruction. Whether this is true for the range of NCAs in the MENA, remains to be determined. By contrast, notwithstanding the sporadic availability of classes, most enthusiasts of the nature exploitation NCAs—fishing, hunting, trapping, mushrooming gathering—seem to enter their hobby by way of informal instruction from friends or relatives. I mention the latter two to demonstrate, as I have done earlier, the scope of the nature exploitation NCAs, recognizing, however, that they may have little currency in the MENA.

The routes to the nature appreciation NCAs are the most varied. It appears that rather few people take classes in hiking, snowshoeing, bird-watching, snowmobiling, iceboating, or horseback riding (as opposed to the equestrian events), another set of activities mostly approached informally through friends and relatives. This may also be true for spelunking. But many people do take noncredit adult education classes in skin diving or canoeing through a college or university department of leisure or physical education. In all the participation activities there is no shortage (at least in English) of books and magazines advising on how and where to do them. Depending on the activity, look for printed material as well as expert advice in sporting goods stores, fishing and hunting suppliers, back-country suppliers, and equestrian suppliers. Finally, remember to check the relevant holdings in the public library and the many Internet sites.

Noncompetitive Activity Participation (Corporeal Activities)

Whereas many of the NCAs just discussed require significant physical involvement from participants, the activities covered in this section are physical, but fail to challenge nature. All have their competitive sides, which when pursued, forces their reclassification as a sport or contest (see next section).

ballroom dancing
gymnastics, tumbling, and acrobatics
ice skating (done on prepared surfaces) and roller skating (including inline)
swimming

Adults entering the corporeal activities of swimming and gymnastics for routine exercise usually take classes at a public or private pool or gym. By contrast, roller skating (including inline skating), and body building are often learned on one's own, perhaps with a modicum of advice from a friend or relative or magazines, books, or online sources. Body building is often undertaken at the YMCA and the YWCA, or search for providers in such categories as "Body Building" or "Health Clubs and Centers" in the MENA Yellow Pages. Note, too, that classes in these activities are sometimes available through one of the adult education programs.

Sports, Games, and Contests

The chief difference separating these participants from the activity participants in the preceding section is the presence of the most essential component of any sport, game, or contest: competition. Both types of hobby are organized according to sets of rules but, in sports, games, and contests, these rules are invariably stated in formal terms—in rule books or on printed sheets—designed to control competitive action in a host of specific ways. The sports are presented here according to their classification as team or individual. Descriptions of each can be found in the larger encyclopedias.

croquet
curling
darts
dog racing (including dog sled racing)
handball (see individual sports, elite amateur)
ice boating racing
lacrosse
long-distance running
martial arts (see individual sports, elite amateur)
model racing (model boats, cars, trucks, airplanes, etc.)
orienteering
polo
pool/billiards/snooker
power boat racing

race walking
shooting (see individual sports, elite amateur)
table tennis (ping-pong)

Nearly all the team and individual sports considered in this section can be played with at least minor satisfaction after a modicum of on-the-spot instruction from an experienced player. The exceptions to this generalization are polo and the martial arts, two sports with major conditioning and background skills that impede immediate participation. Otherwise, entry is comparatively easy, providing beginners can find someone to teach them the rudiments of the sport and indicate some places where he or she may compete in it. Apart from reading a book on the sport in question, the strategy mentioned earlier of hanging around the scene is a common way to become involved (e.g., pool rooms, race tracks, playing fields). Watch for notices of competitions in the sections of the newspaper devoted to sports and community events. Moreover, the players of some of these sports are organized in clubs (see the Yellow Pages under "Clubs"), and there may be an adult education program offering classes in some of them. Finally, the beginner can sometimes start his or her own scene by purchasing a dart set, croquet set, or pool table and inviting friends in for a game or two.

Games, Puzzles, and Mazes

The following list is unabashedly Western. But to list and describe all the world's games and puzzles would amount to a book in itself. The main popular and traditional games of the MENA have already been described. This section adds to this list of games, puzzles, and mazes of possible interest to people seeking some new leisure as well as some suggestions on how to get started in it.

backgammon
card games (bridge, cribbage, poker and blackjack, rummy, solitaire, etc.)
charades
chess and checkers
dice games
dominoes
puzzles, mazes, and brain twisters (including crosswords)
role-playing games
scrabble

The suggestions above for becoming involved in darts, croquet, and the like are more universally applicable to the various games designed for two or more players. In other words, beginners may start their own bridge or poker group or establish with interested partners regular playing sessions of chess, scrabble, Monopoly, or gin rummy. Alternatively, a would-be player may be able to get started in bridge through an adult education class. If the role-playing games have appeal, for example, search for a club devoted to one or more of them. Since these clubs are common on university campuses, ask the office of the student president for information about them. Finally, note that some of the games, such as charades and Pictionary, make good party activities, because they can involve everyone who is present.

The remaining games and all the puzzles are easy to learn and enjoy alone. Some are now available on the more recent Mac and Windows computers. The beginner need only click on the application or turn on a video, follow instructions, shuffle the cards, and deal a hand of solitaire.[35] It is much the same for puzzles, mazes, and brain twisters. As before the foregoing list shows the scope of this kind of leisure, some varieties of which may be unknown to people in the MENA.

The Liberal Arts Hobbies

These pursuits were defined and described in chapter 2, where I also distinguished between fans (casual leisure participants) and buffs (serious leisure participants). With a few exceptions, the participants in the liberal arts hobbies also pursue their leisure as a solitary activity. For this reason a beginner here seldom needs much advice on how to get started. Since reading is the main way of learning in these hobbies, this person simply starts exploring the relevant sections of the community's libraries and bookstores with the goal of building the broad, profound, nontechnical knowledge so highly prized by this type of hobbyist. Novices should be alert for material with which to augment their reading, particularly public talks, audio and video documentaries, and the availability of a multitude of online sources.

And, for the participant who can afford them, trips taken as part of an educational travel program can also significantly augment knowledge and understanding in the geographic-based liberal arts hobbies. A number of universities have noncredit, educational travel programs. They are similar to the Elderhostel Program (USA) and the University of the Third Age Program (UK), which are composed of, among other offerings, one- to two-week noncredit courses presently offered in over forty countries. These educational travel programs well exemplify tourist-based, self-directed education in the liberal arts that, in the cases of Elderhostel and the University of the Third Age, have special appeal for people no longer fully employed and no longer having parental responsibility. In addition to these programs, several partly organized cultural tours exist, many of which are described online under such titles as "learning vacations" and "cultural travel." A set of private tour companies rounds out the cultural touring possibilities for the liberal arts hobbyist (see "Travel Services," "Travel Agents," and similar headings in the main MENA city Yellow Pages). Here, too, since I, as an outsider, could find nothing, interested people within the MENA will have to explore on their own for local equivalents of Elderhostel and the like.

Unlike the other liberal arts hobbyists, people learning a new language inspired by the hope of advancing to a level where they can easily read and speak it, must participate in a profound way in one of the social worlds of the people fluent in that tongue. Consequently, entering this hobby is anything but a solitary activity. Furthermore, it is an interest shared by many people in the MENA, as it is in other parts of the world.

What I observed about how Anglophones learned French in the Canadian city of Calgary (Stebbins 1994b) can be helpful to people in the MENA interested in learning a foreign tongue while living in one of its larger cities. Modeled on the Calgary example, students of a foreign language in the MENA might begin by taking noncredit language courses offered by the Berlitz School of Languages (available in many of the larger cities in the MENA, though not in Iran), an adult education program, or a college or university department of the language in question. Once linguistic fluency has improved sufficiently, some of the students may want to deepen their involvement in the local social world of the language by frequenting its clubs, bookstores, cinemas, restaurants, travel agencies, festivals, and special events. In turn, these contacts can engender a small but expanding number of foreign-language friendships, acquaintanceships, and network connections. For some, those same contacts can also lead to opportunities to work as volunteers for one or two of the foreign-language services in their city. Other students with time and financial means might want to achieve the same end by immersing themselves in a foreign community where the local language dominates, such as London (for English) and Paris (for French).

Volunteer Work as Community Involvement

It is by way of volunteering that community involvement is most obviously realized, the amateur-hobbyist route to this kind of activity commonly being more subtle. Further, in general among the three types of serious leisure, volunteer work offers the easiest entry. A would-be volunteer need only select an area listed below and then contact one of the organizations or types of organizations mentioned there to see if it is looking for the sort of help this person is willing and able to provide. In many instances little advanced preparation is necessary, since most organizations, having specialized roles to fill, prefer to conduct their own training to ensure success (more later on this subject).

The Scope of Volunteering

The following list of areas of volunteer work shows the enormous scope of volunteering, which touches virtually all spheres of every-day life. Here careers in serious leisure volunteering can be pursued through formal activity (working within an organization or association) or through informal activity (working with friends or neighbors or working with a small group, such as a club or self-help group). Some volunteer careers combine both types.

Most volunteering opportunities are of the service variety; the volunteers offer needed help to a specified clientele. But there are also managerial posts for volunteers, among them the team captain of a unit of volunteer firefighters or the coordinator of volunteers in a residence for the elderly. Finally, a small number of all volunteer workers wind up in decision-making positions as members of boards of directors or executive committees.

Bear in mind that simple membership in a club or voluntary association is not itself volunteering, not even casual volunteering. Being on a membership list is not an activity. Members who regularly attend meetings can be considered volunteers, however, to the extent they participate actively in the group's affairs. Whether their volunteering is of the career variety or the casual variety depends on the nature of their participation. The secretary and treasurer are most certainly career volunteers, whereas the rank-and-file who regularly attend the meetings but have only a superficial interest in the issues discussed on the floor are best defined as casual volunteers.

The areas of volunteering examined below are mostly illustrated with Western, often North American, examples. It is a serious weakness that I am unable to provide examples from the MENA, for it is my intention in this section, as in those preceding it, to encourage volunteering among its people. Nonetheless, these people, in reading this chapter, will learn about what is happening in the West and then, hopefully, try to find in these opportunities or import them with appropriate adaptations to their own countries.

Provision of Necessities

The necessities provided are food, shelter, clothing, and other basic goods and services. The Islamic *Qurbani* W*aqf* (provides meat) and Emergency Relief Waqf (provides food, shelter, medicine, blankets) along with local food banks (there is one operating in Egypt under this title) number among the organizations using volunteers to serve the poor (the Goodwill Industries and the Salvation Army, though they operate in many developing countries, are not found in the MENA). Some volunteers, who provide necessities, collect used clothing and household items, some repair these items once they are collected, some distribute the restored items to the needy. Other volunteers work in the hostels and missions providing shelter to the homeless. Volunteers also prepare the meals served to the indigent or deliver already prepared meals to a home-bound clientele, possibly by way of a service in the MENA similar to that of Meals on Wheels in Canada, Australia, the United Kingdom, and the United States.

Education

Some educational volunteers work under a teacher's supervision tutoring students with problems in such areas as reading, spelling, and mathematics. Alternatively, these volunteers help organize and run field trips and extracurricular activities. To the extent that it is substantial and enduring, work for the school's Parent-Teacher Association (PTA) can also be considered educational volunteering. There are PTAs in several MENA countries, some of which are affiliated with Western schools and some of which are affiliated with Arab institutions. Additionally, people skilled in a foreign language are sometimes invited to help students polish their linguistic accents, oral delivery, and reception of the tongue, a service that includes teaching immigrants English as a second language. Organizations such as Literacy Volunteers of America and Laubach Literacy Action have the goal of promoting competence in English for all. Look for their equivalents in the MENA. And a volunteer, perhaps most commonly a parent, occasionally augments the coaching staff of one of the school's interscholastic sports. In some communities the school bus drivers work gratis, and volunteers with sufficient background are used to instruct school dropouts in trade skills like printing, textile work, woodworking, and metal machining. Volunteers are also needed to teach the repair of the many items of equipment and products, such as lathes and looms. Finally, volunteer teachers may be invited to teach the repair of textiles, paper products (e.g., books), and products made of sand, glass, stone, and clay.

Science

Scientific volunteers sometimes collaborate with the schools, where they help organize and run science fairs and long-term classroom projects in the physical and biological sciences. Others, as mentioned earlier, are amateurs converted to volunteer public relations officers for their sciences, as seen in their efforts to educate the general public in the fundamentals of the discipline and lobby the government for favorable legislation. In addition, volunteers are contracted as guides to serve in such establishments as zoos, museums, arboretums, planetariums, and botanical gardens. Finally, they may be given specific volunteer tasks in certain scientific research projects. Here they fill the role of assistant, thereby distinguishing themselves from the more autonomous amateur scientists mentioned earlier. The Earthwatch Institute, an international service with offices in many parts of the world, organizes such help for a number of these projects; its mission is to recruit volunteers to work in professional research in art, archaeology, and marine studies, as well as in the geosciences, life sciences, and social sciences. Unfortunately, according to its website, the MENA has been completely overlooked by this group, either as a target of its expeditions or as a location for a branch institute.[36]

Civic Affairs

Civic affairs cover an extremely broad area, even though it excludes politics, a separate field considered below. In general, volunteering in civic affairs entails working in a community-level service or project, most probably one sponsored by government. Thus volunteers are recruited for certain municipal services, including government-run historical sites, an assortment of special projects (e.g., World's Fair, Olympic Games, major arts festivals), and the many programs in tourism and sports and fitness. Here volunteers serve as tour guides, staff visitor information booths, and work in programs for youth or seniors. They are also invited to help maintain tourist sites and public grounds. Some volunteers find work at the public library; others become involved in neighborhood crime or fire prevention. Those with appropriate skills and experience may be asked to write brochures, historical material, even technical documents. The branches of municipal government with the greatest thirst for volunteers are, first, the branch concerned with parks, leisure, and recreation and, second, the one responsible for social services.

Health

Volunteer work in health is restricted by the jurisdictional controls of such professions as nursing and medicine. Nonetheless, volunteers with appropriate certification are engaged to teach first-aid courses and present public lectures on health-related issues. In hospitals and private homes, they feed people who have trouble feeding themselves; provide company for lonely patients by way of reading and conversation; and work to retrain the temporarily disabled by helping them swim, walk, and otherwise move their atrophied limbs. Despite these many services, health volunteers are possibly most active in the physical fitness arena, where they guide exercise sessions in yoga, aerobics, and similar activities. Finally, these volunteers are needed for work with the mentally disordered and physically disabled to help them adapt to life in the wider community. Some provide transportation for these people using specially designed vehicles. Relevant North American organizations here include the Senior Companion Program, Grey Panthers, and Citizen Action, in addition to a sizeable number of disease-specific organizations concerned with cancer, heart disease, Alzheimer's disease, and the like. There are probably similar groups in the MENA.

Economic Development

Opportunities for volunteering in this area are nearly innumerable. For one, volunteers fill diverse roles in the many organizations providing help or relief in the developing world. In this regard, some volunteers solicit money for CARE, Oxfam, or the Red Cross, whereas others serve as clerks, managers, or secretaries in these organizations. Some American volunteers go overseas with the Peace Corps to work directly with local people by helping them build a school or an irrigation system, for example, or establishing an effective nutritional program. People with the appropriate training may find it satisfying to work abroad for Volunteers in Overseas Cooperative Assistance or Volunteers in Technical Assistance. Back home, volunteers with an entrepreneurial background—often retirees—advise on ways to get new businesses off the ground or help those that are floundering to survive (e.g., Service Corps of Retired Executives). Volunteers in Service to America (now called AmeriCorps VISTA) work to revitalize low-income rural, urban, and native individuals and their communities.

Even while certain areas of the MENA are occasionally the target of benefits from groups like Oxfam and the Red Cross, local Arabs and Iranians may also volunteer their services with them. Retired business people in the MENA, who would like to help start new businesses or advise existing ones in financial trouble, should look for counterparts to the organizations listed in the preceding paragraph or, if unavailable, start one of their own.

Physical Environment

Some people in this area volunteer to enhance public lands, lakes, and streams by planting trees or caring for lawns and flower gardens. Others devote their after work time to improving the execution of an outdoor activity, such as cleaning up beaches, beautifying picnic grounds, clearing hiking and skiing trails, or removing refuse and dead-fall from trout streams. Sports and environmentalist groups (e.g., the Sierra Club) rely heavily on volunteers to conduct publicity campaigns about their programs and concerns as well as to try to persuade the government to stop certain practices inimical to the environment or a particular outdoor sport. One major consumer of volunteer time in this area is the United States Forest Service Volunteers Program. The American Hiking Society Volunteer Vacations organization does similar work. Volunteers also teach in state- or province-run programs designed to instruct youth in outdoor skills and responsible use of natural resources. In the MENA, explore the Yellow Pages with terms such as "Environmental Organizations" to locate clubs and associations interested in recruiting volunteers to work for them.

Religion

There is a great variety of volunteer activities for people desiring to work within the ambit of one of the many religious organizations in operation today. Volunteers in this area are used to organize and run social events and charity campaigns, as well as fill lay roles in religious services. Many churches are organized, in part, according to committees, which are staffed mainly, if not entirely, with volunteers. In addition, volunteers are used extensively to distribute literature and disseminate information about their religion. They work in religion-specific information centers (e.g., the Christian Science Reading Rooms), staff telephone information lines, and hand out brochures and booklets. An Internet search using the terms "Islamic Volunteers" and "Muslim Volunteers" uncovered a wide reliance on volunteers in Islamic programs in many parts of the world. But does Islamic volunteering exist within the MENA? Here the World Wide Web is silent (at least in English and French).

Volunteering within religion may also take the form of spiritual development, or lay religious counseling and education. This area is as diverse as the many religions operating in the modern world. Friendly visiting, at times of death, disaster, or severe illness, is an example. Missionary work belongs here, to the extent that it is satisfying and neither coerced nor substantially remunerated. Teaching Christian Sunday school or its equivalent in other religions and leading adult discussion groups also contribute to spiritual development. Most opportunities for volunteering in this area appear to come through a religious establishment, that is, either a religious movement or a religious organization.

Politics

As mentioned earlier, community involvement in the sphere of politics is often discussed under the heading of citizen participation. It appears that most political volunteers work for a political party, for which they disseminate information about its platform and candidates by carrying banners, posting notices, canvassing door-to-door, distributing party literature, and so on. These people are joined by other volunteers at local meetings of the party, where they choose election candidates, hammer out campaign strategies, and organize publicity drives. Moreover, it tends to fall to the volunteers to recruit new members to the party and raise funds for its operation. Finally, some of the most faithful and committed party members are elected as delegates to state, provincial, and national conventions.

Outside the framework of the political parties lie hundreds of special-interest groups, entities run almost entirely by volunteers. They are political inasmuch as they hope either to change government policy or to preserve the status quo. Organizations in the United States like Common Cause strive to ensure good government, while those such as Project Vote and the League of Women Voters work to generate maximum voter participation at the polls. In all these groups, the appetite for help in lobbying the government and informing the voters is nearly insatiable. Still another genre of political volunteering is that done for such organizations as the American Civil Liberties Union and the Canadian Civil Liberties Association.

But all this is about volunteering in democratic societies. How relevant is it to the MENA? Here according to the "The Economist Intelligence Unit's Index of Democracy 2010" there is not one democracy to be found, not even a "flawed democracy." (Lebanon is classified as a "hybrid regime" and the rest as "authoritarian regimes.")[37] People inside the MENA will know the answer to this question much better than I, an outsider. But should the Arab Spring result eventually in democracy of some kind in some countries, the role of the political volunteer, as described above, will become important.

Government

Volunteers here work in programs and services run by a branch of a municipal, county, state, provincial, or federal government. Volunteer firefighters and emergency service workers (in, for example, first-aid, disaster relief, and search-and-rescue) exemplify well voluntary action in this area. I have noted the trend in some urban police forces toward using volunteers to staff citizen patrols and operate neighborhood crime prevention programs (Stebbins, 1992). Volunteers are also widely employed in the entire range of youth and seniors' programs. Additionally, some judicial systems recruit volunteers to work with parolees as well as provide various kinds of assistance in courtrooms.

Safety

This is the classificatory home of those volunteers who work to prevent violence and disorderly conduct in the schools and on the playgrounds. Adult school-patrol guards constitute another example, as do groups formed to prevent bullying on educational sites. The Guardian Angels, a nonviolent volunteer organization dedicated to restoring order to urban streets and transportation systems, is a community-wide form of safety volunteering found in many of the larger cities in fifteen countries.[38] None of them is in the MENA.

Human Relationships

This area embraces the volunteer work centered on establishing and maintaining a long-term relationship between a child and an adult or between two adults. Examples include the ties established through the exchange-student programs linking students with their host families and through the youth programs linking troubled adolescents with adult mentors (on mentoring as a genre of volunteering, see Stebbins [2006]). Volunteers serving in the Big Brothers and Big Sisters programs[39] develop similar ties with their clients. The welcoming programs for new residents are organized around the formation of interpersonal relationships between newcomers to the community and established local residents. Finally, a variety of social services are provided by volunteers working closely with individual clients over a period of time. These services are delivered in such places as women's shelters, centers for runaway teenagers, and halfway houses and reintegration programs for reforming alcoholics, drug users, and newly released prisoners. In the MENA, for example, in February 2007, the Government of Jordan opened the Family Reconciliation House for abused women.[40] Other volunteer services of this type are made available through parental aid programs and aid programs for children and seniors. In September 2011, I examined the membership list of the International Society for Third Sector Research, which revealed organizations and services in this area in Bahrain, Iran, Lebanon, Jordan, Kuwait, Yemen, Morocco, and Saudi Arabia. Their presence belies the culture obstacle of corporate weakness and, to the extent that everyone in need is served, that of fissiparousness/oppositionalism as well.

The Arts

This area of volunteering centers primarily on the needs of local and regional arts groups. Groups in dance, music, and theater often need help in making costumes, constructing sets, writing programs, and publicizing performances. These groups are amateur by and large, since the professionals tend to rely on paid equivalents. Still, some amateur groups and many professional groups are governed by volunteer boards of directors. Furthermore, there is a voracious appetite for volunteers to help with the operation of the various annual arts festivals, the planning and execution of which span much of the year. The individual arts of painting and craft work, for example, although less dependent on volunteers than the collective arts, nevertheless routinely solicit their help in publicizing and staffing exhibitions and in writing the materials announcing their dates and locations. National Public Radio in Washington D.C. uses volunteers to answer its telephones, operate its computers, prepare mailings, post newspaper clippings, and organize and conduct tours of its facilities.

Recreation

Some of the activities of recreational volunteers were covered earlier under the headings of education, government, and civic affairs. Beyond these spheres, this type of volunteer can be found organizing and running events at the different sports clubs and unaffiliated annual sports competitions so common these days in running, cycling, canoe racing, and cross-country ski racing, to mention a few. Adult volunteers serve as referees for most child and adolescent sports contests, and even some involving adults. Elsewhere, volunteer recreational workers perform a diversity of functions at many of the summer camps for children and adolescents. Those who work with the Cubs Scouts, Boy Scouts, Girl Guides, and similar organizations are, for the most part, recreational volunteers. Many nations in the MENA have Scout Organizations. In addition, there are volunteers who work with children as story tellers. Finally, volunteer ushers for plays, games, shows, and concerts are most accurately placed in this category.

Support Services

The large majority of volunteer activities considered so far are formal; each is carried out within the framework of at least one organization or association. Running an organization is itself a complicated, time-consuming undertaking in which volunteers can fill a variety of important support roles. Thus, in all these areas, volunteer help is also routinely sought for clerical and secretarial duties. In many areas a need also exists for bookkeeping and accounting services, a support activity that a volunteer can often provide. To the extent the activity is managed and administered from a nondomestic site, a volunteer may be engaged to do janitorial work or maintain the grounds around the building.

Informal Volunteering

To qualify as serious leisure, informal volunteer work for friends or neighbors must be regular and substantial. Regularly volunteering to babysit a child, care for a pet, clean a friend's house, or do a neighbor's yard work are some current examples. Participating regularly and substantially in the affairs of a small club or self-help group is a well-known form of informal volunteering, as is working with one of the "anonymous" groups—Debtors Anonymous, Gamblers Anonymous, Neurotics Anonymous, Alcoholics Anonymous, and so on. A number of small clubs and societies engage in informal volunteering, by

135

offering a specialized service, such as cleaning up roadsides, helping street children, or developing and disseminating views on, say, the uses of or policies about a nearby park, lake, or river. Local chapters of the Society for the Prevention of Cruelty to Animals (SPCA) offer an opportunity for informal volunteering by people concerned about the welfare of urban pets. The SPCA is found in many countries around the world, although not presently in the MENA, at least not by that name.

Conclusions

It is impossible to list all the types of volunteering found in any one of the areas presented above. The types are simply too numerous to include in the present book, especially when at the same time, new ones are frequently emerging, inspired, as many are, by the ever deeper reach of electronic technology and its relentless march across the planet. Considering the range of activities covered to this point, what is conspicuous is the scope of serious leisure in North America and, more generally, the West. Hopefully that discussion will enable anyone in the MENA, with an interest in a particular category and sufficient understanding of the activities possibly available there, to initiate his or her own search for opportunities to pursue them.

Some of the areas of career volunteering considered in this chapter require significant amounts of training. Indeed some, including many in education, require full certification of the volunteer, even though he or she is working without pay. Obviously, these areas are open only to specialists who have retired or occupational devotees who find their work too exciting to abandon in their free time. Yet, it is fortunate that entry into the large majority of the aforementioned activities is substantially less restrictive than these specialized fields.

It is also obvious that some of the activities just discussed lend themselves to either casual involvement or serious involvement. In volunteering that depends on the demands made on the volunteer. For instance, a clear difference exists in the ability and experience required to coordinate a canoe race consisting of scores of contestants and that required to ensure that each pair of paddlers is properly registered. The first is an instance of career volunteering, whereas the second is an instance of casual volunteering. But, clearly, both types of volunteering are often needed if the overall activity is be implemented effectively. Career volunteering offers many more enduring rewards than its casual cousin, but both kinds are common and occasionally indispensable for the same activity.

In short, casual volunteering can be absolutely crucial to a larger volunteer project or activity. Even though it requires minimal skill, knowledge, or experience, it is undeniably community involvement. As such it can be significantly satisfying leisure for the participant. Yet the nature of this satisfaction differs profoundly from the nature of the satisfaction found in career volunteering. The satisfaction gained from career volunteering comes from experiencing the special rewards exclusively available in all three types of serious leisure, rewards unavailable in casual volunteering, in particular, or in casual leisure, in general.

There are some important fragments of advice to add to the preceding discussion of volunteering. First, it seems that, throughout the world, many cities of medium size or larger have some sort of central clearinghouse for volunteers, a service on which people may draw for information about the wide range of groups and organizations perpetually in need of volunteers. These agencies usually go by the title of "volunteer center" or "voluntary action center," but according to the brief consideration of the matter in chapter 4, these are uncommon in the MENA. Moreover, most community-oriented newspapers publish a section every week or two detailing the volunteer needs at the moment of any organization in the area who informs the periodical of their situation. Community radio and television stations sometimes offer a similar service. Note, too, as a possible model to follow, that web-based national clearinghouses for volunteers now exist in many countries in the West. Finally, there are also a variety of self-help volunteer data banks; their aim being to organize specialized services for the members of particular demographic categories as rendered by the members themselves (e.g., women, Muslims, the elderly, an ethnic group). For example, the American Association of Retired Persons (AARP) maintains such a data bank, which however, only serves certain categories of clients older than fifty, the minimum age for AARP membership. Members of AARP supply these services.

This chapter has centered on the practical side of the leisure pursuits and community involvement. It has, of necessity, been detailed in scope. The next chapter continues with this approach, showing how leisure and work can be brutal, thereby increasing significantly the complexity of their roles in cultural development and community involvement.

Notes

33. Source: http://www.toastmasters.org, retrieved 3 September 2011.
34. Source: http://www.ediforma.net, retrieved 30 August 2011.
35. There are hundreds of these games, see http://www.solitairegames.com, retrieved 3 September 2011.
36. Source: http://www.earthwatch.org, retrieved 3 September 2011.
37. Source: http://graphics.eiu.com/PDF/Democracy_Index_2010_web.pdf, retrieved 4 September 2011.
38. Source: http://www.guardianangels.org/chapters.php, retrieved 4 September 2011.
39. Now operating in thirteen countries, http://www.bbbsi.org, retrieved 4 September 2011.
40. Source: http://www.freedomhouse.org/modules/publications/ccr/mod-PrintVersion.cfm?edition=9&ccrpage=43&ccrcountry=189, retrieved 12 September 2011.

6

Serious Pursuits of the Brutal Kind

We have thus far examined in the MENA what might be called its "normal" leisure, leisure that, though constrained at times by various politico-religious forces, consists of activities that ordinary Arabs and Iranians actually do or could see themselves doing. In other words, were circumstances right—had they sufficient time, money, taste, talent, and access—they could see themselves pursuing those activities. Such leisure is normal because, within these limits, it appeals to large segments of the population and because they view it as morally and socially acceptable. True, people who identify strongly with the politico-religious constraints have a narrower zone of acceptability—of normal leisure—than those who want to push beyond these confines. This has been discussed as subversive leisure at various points in the preceding chapters.

Nevertheless, there is another angle from which to understand how people choose their leisure, namely, by studying its facilitators (Raymore 2002), as opposed to the constraints discussed in the preceding paragraph. In particular, what role does Arab-Iranian culture play in encouraging its people to go in for certain kinds of free-time activities? We have already examined several manifestations of this line of influence in normal leisure, evident in the distinctive Middle Eastern arts, sport, scientific, and entertainment fields. Several kinds of casual leisure have also been shown to be facilitated by the culture of the region.

It is important to note, however, that there is in the MENA a notorious set of leisure pursuits of considerable profundity that is anything but normal. Not normal, yes, but still encouraged and for that reason facilitated by the local culture. One group of these activities, referred to here as *brutal leisure*, may be classified as either serious leisure or devotee work, where sometimes a leisure career from the first to the second is possible. The activities considered in this chapter under that heading are terrorism, assassination, religious-based violence, revolutionary violence, some police work, and some of the military occupations. Such activities are also highly dangerous, mainly because their targets try hard to oppose them by employing their own versions of brutality or, at the very least, by threatening apprehension and imprisonment. For example, security personnel at foreign embassies have orders to shoot to kill terrorists attempting to blow up their buildings or assassinate their officials.

This chapter examines the above-mentioned six types of brutal leisure, but not without a preamble bearing on the differences between it and deviant leisure as seen through the prism of the MENA.

Deviant and Brutal Leisure in the MENA

The concept of deviant leisure was set out in chapter 2, defined there as a contravention of the moral norms of a society that frame leisure behavior. One key difference separating deviant and brutal leisure is precisely this, its place along the moral dimension. Just how immoral is brutal leisure in the MENA when directed, for example, against national enemies (e.g., Israel, United States) or hated religious groups (e.g., Coptic Christians in Egypt, Sunnis in Iraq)? Jihad, for instance, which is a religious duty for some devout Muslims, includes the duty to struggle to defend the faith. (Two other jihad-prescribed duties are the struggle to keep the faith and the struggle to improve Islamic society.) The first struggle, the one of defense, justifies brutality where necessary and, among believers in Islamic circles, is an act of conformity rather than deviance.

In chapter 2 we considered as serious pursuits aberrant religion, politics, and science engaged in as appealing but morally wrong work or leisure. Deviant religion is exemplified by the diverse sects and cults found in the typical modern society, while deviant politics is looked on in the wider community as activity undertaken in service of the goal of nondemocratic, often violent, overthrow of the established government or system of government. Yet, what is moral and immoral varies from culture to culture, sometimes widely. The six activities in this chapter are felt in some parts of the MENA to be acceptable, even while they are also dangerous to life and limb of the participants. Such bravery is honorable in the eyes of these people, a judgment they may anchor in their interpretation of the Qur'an.

I know of no English or French data describing the demographic distribution of people in the MENA (i.e., by sex, religion, education) who define as deviant particular acts of terrorism against say, the United States, military suppression of a local insurgency, or bombing of a mosque serving a detested Islamic denomination. Given this lack, all that may be claimed in the present chapter is that for some people such acts are acceptable, for some others tolerably deviant, and for still some others intolerably deviant. From the standpoint of leisure studies, however, these acts, unless the actors have been conscripted or otherwise coerced against their will to perpetrate them, may be conceptualized as leisure of the brutal kind. Moreover, because significant skill, knowledge, and experience are typically required to engage in them, they constitute either serious leisure or devotee work, the latter designation being valid when these participants find all or a part of livelihood in the activity. As serious leisure (and not work) they may be conceived of as either career or project-based volunteering. In all cases they must therefore be understood as another class of cultural development and community involvement, as twisted as this classification may seem to Western sensibilities.

Brutal leisure is hardly limited to the contemporary MENA. The history of humanity is bursting with instances of it, although in modern times, the rate of such violence is now much less (Pinker 2011). Nevertheless, its further reduction poses a major challenge. Rape is a main type; it is still very much a part of all modern-day societies. Police brutality occasionally makes the headlines in the West, as in other parts of the world. Annual homicide rates are calculated in all cities, with the most violent being given the title of "murder capital." Serial killing has been studied as leisure. (For papers on serial murder and violence done for "fun," see the special issue of *Leisure/Loisir*, v. 30, no. 1, 2006.) Despite this scenario and according to World Life Expectancy, the MENA has been following the global tendency, most of it today containing some of the world's least violent societies.[41]

The remainder of this chapter will be devoted to adducing evidence in support of the observation that brutal serious pursuits are still sometimes pursued within the MENA, as well as by Arabs and Iranians operating outside their home region. Moreover, given the upheaval associated with the Arab Spring, the rates of internal violence since it commenced in December 2010 may well turn out to be significantly higher than earlier. Indeed, it is now difficult to see countries in the throes of the Arab Spring as anything other than violent, even while there are undoubtedly tranquil areas in each.

Terrorist Activities

Terrorist activities are intimidating and at times downright brutal, often being driven by the goal of coercing a government or community to accede to particular ideological demands. In some contemporary terrorist acts, however, the demands are vague, even nonexistent, being designed primarily to sow fear and unease in the target population. No change is intended here. But how can such violent undertakings be regarded as leisure?

First, let us be clear that it seems highly improbable that people engaging in brutal leisure of the kind discussed in this chapter, even while it is uncoerced, actually see it as leisure. This is the commonsense view. Using the SLP, however, it is possible to explain terrorist acts as a genre of serious pursuit. Terrorists, to the extent that they use homemade bombs, must know how to acquire the requisite materials, put them together such that they will explode with the ruinous consequences hoped for, place them for optimum effectiveness, and escape detection. The suicide bomber, of course, cares not at all about this final bit of knowledge. But, for all terrorists, all this requires a great deal of planning, bringing to the fore another element of sophistication in this kind of brutal leisure. If terrorism comes in the form of biological and chemical brutality, then the terrorists must know when, where, and how to use these substances to good effect and without getting caught. Such activity demands a lot of time from the terrorist, suggesting that funding must be found to support his or her more or less full-time efforts. Getting funded is yet another aspect of the knowledge base of this kind of brutal leisure. The terrorists who flew the planes into the twin towers of the World Trade Center in September of 2001 had spent many hours learning how to fly passenger jets.

Effort, acquisition of skill and knowledge, and perseverance are among the quintessential qualities of the serious pursuits. They engender a sense of leisure career as the participant develops along these lines. In these pursuits, rewarding outcomes abound, including in terrorism, the devastation brought about by the bombing, poisoning, killing, and so on. Then there is the rich leisure social world of the terrorist, consisting of a network of like-minded others, suppliers of equipment, sympathetic collaborators, and enthusiastic funders, to mention a few. In such circles it is an honor to be identified as a terrorist (local nomenclature may well be less pejorative) or to be identified as a committed participant in brutal leisure given over to advancing a popular cause or grievance.

Consider as an example the National Counterterrorism Center in the United States and its lists and descriptions of the range of methods and tactics that may be used in terrorist undertakings.[42] Here you will find a short discussion of "bomb threat stand-off distances" or evacuation distances according to different types of bomb. The properties of many different kinds of lethal chemicals are also set out. The website further describes what to watch for in phony documents, notably passports. There is also a section on TNT and comparable explosives complete with their names and related pressure and impulse equivalents. Successful terrorists must be knowledgeable of much or all of these dimensions of their hobby or occupation. If they travel outside their country, they must know how create false passports that will escape detection. If this be leisure for them, it is certainly of the serious variety.

Assassinations

Assassination is the planned murder of someone, usually a public figure. The very fact that assassinations must be planned places them, to the extent that they are leisure for the assassin, in the category of serious pursuits. As a case in point, look at Mohammed Bouyeri, who in November 2004, assassinated Theo Van Gogh, prominent Dutch film director. The act was motivated by the latter's depiction in his television film *Submission* some of the extremes of Islam. According to Glen Frankel, a journalist for the *Washington Post*:

> Bouyeri "spent a lot of time hanging out on the streets" of Amsterdam and at some point "was arrested and imprisoned for seven months" for a violent crime. It is believed that during his incarceration, Bouyeri immersed himself in the teachings of Islam.... It is unclear if he took on a new job but what is known is that he devoted a large portion of his daily life to religious activities after he left the organization. Bouyeri formed new friendships at this time with other men who shared similar extremist views. One person who Bouyeri befriended was Samir Azzouz, 18, an Islamic fundamentalist who was arrested in the Netherlands for plotting bomb attacks on Amsterdam's Schiphol Airport and the Dutch Parliament, Expatica.com reported in a November 3, 2004 article. Bouyeri was believed to also have formed friendships with other dangerous Islamic extremists who were under watch by the government.... During this time, Bouyeri also joined a militant Islamic group known as the Hofstad

Network. Syrian-born geologist turned spiritual leader, Redouan al-Issar, 43, also known to use the alias "Abu Kaled," headed the group. Even though Bouyeri's first known act of terrorism in association with the Hofstad Network was the murder of Theo Van Gogh, it is believed that he and the group were also in the process of plotting even more assassinations. The group's suspected targets included Ayaan Hirsi Ali and right-wing conservative MP Geert Wilders who, according to an October 2004 Expatica.com article, is known to be "unashamedly anti-Islam."[43]

This passage, which describes several facets of Bouyeri's social world and his immersion in the teachings of Islam, attests the serious leisure nature of his activities. Given the list of assassination targets, we may conclude that he also envisioned a career in this hobby. Was he paid? Was this in fact devotee work? There appears to be no evidence on this question, though it would be possible in the Netherlands to subsist for some time on welfare payments. Alternatively, like many a fine artist and struggling entertainer, he could have managed working part-time in manual labor or in the service industry.

Religious-Based Violence

Down through history religious-based violence has occurred as two major types: intra- and interfaith brutality. Exemplifying the intrafaith type in Christianity, observe how Catholics and Protestants have battled each other in Northern Ireland since early in the seventeenth century. In Islam, Sunnis and Shiites, adepts of the two main denominations of that religion, at various points in time since 656, have warred with one another over doctrinal differences. Brutal conflict between them has been intense in, for example, Iraq since the start in 2003 of the US-Iraq war. There are further examples on the interfaith plane. Here Christians battled Muslims during the Crusades, which took place in the main between the eleventh and thirteenth centuries. And, since the founding of the Jewish state of Israel in 1948, an act that met with widespread disapproval in the MENA, among other Islamic regions, there have been brutal exchanges. These have taken diverse forms, most notably rocket attacks, suicide bombings, and military incursions on the ground and in the air.

Obviously, the MENA and the larger Arab-Iranian world have no monopoly on either intra- or interfaith violence. Across history, Christians have also been quite active in this way. But, staying with the subject of this book, what kinds of brutal leisure undergird such violence as manifested in the MENA? Halalplaza.com, an Islamic portal designed to inform Muslims about matters of daily life, has this to say about the violent side of the Shiite-Sunni divide:

> The Shiite Sunni divide though [it] existed in the Islamic world has never reached this level before. At this rate of incitement being triggered by both parties, the Sunni Shiite (Shia) hatred is bound to spread throughout the Islamic world. Listening to stories in the media about Sunnis killing Shias and Shiite militias raping Sunni women are just the early sparks of this hatred. This has the potential of sparking local unrest within countries which has a Shiite population. Pakistan, India, Lebanon, Saudi Arabia, Gulf countries and many others have a large Shiite population. Some Arab newspapers have already been reporting about an alleged scheme by Shiite militias to murder Sunni religious leaders. Shiite newspapers mention about similar allegations. Case in point—In November 2006, the Associated Press reported that "A previously unknown extremist group has warned that 'Shiite death squads' acting under Iranian religious edicts are preparing to attack Sunni Muslims in Lebanon." One wonders if it's going to even get better, especially after clerics and some religious leaders within Iraq are promoting direct killings of the other sect.[44]

Nevertheless, Nathan Gonsalez (2009, 8), fellow with the Truman National Security Project, holds that "the vast majority of Muslims do not even give a second thought to their friendship with a member of a different sect." Religious-based brutality may not always be deviant in the MENA; nonetheless it is leisure for only a small minority of the Muslim faithful living in the region.

Revolutionary Violence

The brutality perpetrated during revolutions is intended to further the desire of the revolutionaries to provoke major governmental changes in the target society. As a type of brutality, it is usually broader than the preceding types, even though terrorism, assassination, and religious-based violence may be enacted in the name of revolution. In other words some kinds of revolutionary violence stand apart from these three. Many of the events of the Arab Spring exemplify this kind. As an example, consider sabotage of governmental property and personnel by revolutionary interests. Such activity coming from people living outside the targeted country (or living within it while being estranged from its culture) is usually labeled as terrorist. It becomes revolutionary when done from within by otherwise ordinary citizens who, however, see no effective way to change their society's government other than by brutal recourse. The activity evolves into civil war when those who are fighting comprise sizeable proportions of the society's overall population, with each group bent on forcefully establishing or preserving its own government.

Nir Rosen (2011), writing for *Jadaliyya*, shows how Yemen president Ali Abdallah Salih, whose reign dates to 1978, is trying to control the diverse revolutionary elements active in his country:

> Salih, who rules the poorest Arab country, seems poised to be the next dictator to fall in the popular revolutions spreading from Tunisia on to Egypt. Though each country is different, many of the complaints demonstrators voice are the same, and thanks to al Jazeera and social media, activists are able to learn effective tactics. Yemen today is an uncomfortable amalgam of North Yemen and South Yemen, united in 1990. Yemen receives attention for the small al Qaeda presence but this is the least of its problems. In the north Salih has been brutally fighting Zeydi Shiites seeking autonomy by massively bombing their villages, displacing hundreds of thousands and then attacking displaced civilians. In the south he is at war against secessionists. The peaceful southern movement which demonstrated for a more just access to power and resources was violently crushed, leading some of its members to turn to armed resistance. Salih delegates control over much of the country to tribal sheikhs whose loyalty is tenuous. Yemen's powerful Saudi neighbors are deeply involved in its internal affairs, their money purchasing officials and spreading Wahabi Islam. Salih has instrumentalized al Qaeda against domestic foes while using the threat of al Qaeda to extort money from Americans who see the Muslim world only through the prism of the war on terror.

To the extent that revolutionaries engage in skilled, knowledgeable activity and persevere at it while putting in considerable effort, revolutionary violence too may be considered serious leisure. This assumes, however, that they are thus involved willingly, though most probably pushed by a strong sense of political obligation. "I must take to the streets, but I also want to take to the streets." This is, at bottom, career volunteering to further a communitarian cause. It constitutes a leisure career because revolutions commonly last for a number of years as they pass from armed clashes to establishing a workable new government engineered by the victorious forces. The social world of those who participate in this type of brutal leisure consists of fellow revolutionaries, friendly suppliers of food and munitions, other citizens who support their mission, and the like. The ethos encapsulating their activities is the ideology and associated aims of the revolution.

Their identity is that of someone who supports and works toward such violent social change.

Police and Military Work

The job of the police in authoritarian societies includes ensuring conformity to the laws established and wishes pursued by the dominant regime (i.e., dynasty, army, tribe, etc.). It also includes ensuring tranquility where that group perceives a threat to its dominance, whether from within or outside the society's legal system. That is, these rulers will use whenever necessary illegitimate, extra-legal force, be it the police or, we must now add, the military, to protect their privileged status and interests.

To the extent that members of the police and the military are conscripted against their will to these roles, it is logically difficult to see their activities in them as leisure. Allowing for the possibility that they might come to like their work, including its brutal aspects, they are still initially coerced into it. Others, however, join precisely because the violent side of the work appeals to them, not unlike mercenaries who are volunteer merchants of violence. It also seems reasonable to conclude that those who seek police or military employment identify with its conservative nature, which is to uphold the existing social order as shaped by their employer, the dominant regime Thus both the employees and their employers dislike, even hate anyone threatening this order, and therefore find it easy, even enjoyable, to be brutal toward this threat.

At the same time serving in the police or the military is a paying job. In fact, in many developing countries, it may be one of the most accessible, gainful, stable forms of employment around. It is possible, of course, that some people seek such work primarily because they want the money and not because they enjoy its core activities. But others, also forced to make a living doing something, go in for such work because they *do* enjoy them, in part because it squares with their interests in violence and hatred for the groups in the community or society that the dominant regime wants to control. For this group, theirs is devotee work.

It would seem unnecessary to go into detail about the amount and kind of knowledge, skill, and experience needed to succeed at these devotee occupations. In general they comprise the usual qualifications for police and military work, including the multitude of techniques used to torture people for information, engage in reprisals, or harass disliked segments of the population. In the MENA, serving an authoritarian government that the worker respects against interests that both dislike (e.g., another Islamic denomination, Western involvements, insurgent groups), constitutes a set of agreeable activities profound enough to be stamped as a serious pursuit.

Human Rights Watch, a New York-based independent organization dedicated to defending and protecting human rights, interviewed twenty-five former detainees from the city of Homs in Syria. Their report (Human Rights Watch 2011) describes a sample of the brutal leisure of the military as it attempts to put down insurgent activity there:

> As in much of the rest of Syria, security forces in Homs governorate subjected thousands of people to arbitrary arrests, enforced disappearances, and systematic torture in detention. While most were released after several weeks in detention, several hundred remain missing. Most detainees were young men in their 20s or 30s, but security forces also detained children, women, and elderly people. Several witnesses reported that their parents or even grandparents—people in their 60s and 70s—had been detained.

> Torture of detainees is rampant. Twenty-five former detainees from Homs were among those interviewed by Human Rights Watch. They all reported being subjected to various forms of torture. Human Rights Watch has independently documented 17 deaths in custody in Homs, at least 12 of which were clearly from torture. Data collected by local activists suggest even higher figures. They say that at least 40 people detained in Homs governorate died in custody between April and August.

> Former detainees reported security forces' use of heated metal rods to burn various parts of their bodies, the use of electric shocks, the use of stress positions for hours or even days at a time, and the use of improvised devices, such as car tires (locally known as *dulab*), to force detainees into positions that make it easier to beat them on sensitive parts of the body, like the soles of the feet and head.

For those who find fulfillment there, this is devotee work of the professional variety, in the sense that these workers gain a livelihood of some sort. As amateurs they would have gone through training programs analogous to the formation of student physicians, engineers, and police and military personnel in non-MENA countries. For some people going in for such violence, its appeal is further enhanced when it squares with their ideological leanings. The many defectors from the police and military (media reports of violence in the Arab Spring are replete with mention of them) constitute further evidence that for them their earlier participation in these units was uncoerced leisure. But now its appeal has dramatically declined, such that they want to abandon this pursuit, and indeed have succeeded in doing so. Any dislike they once harbored toward those who threaten the established order has been replaced with sympathy, perhaps even love, exemplified in mid-2012 by defections from President Bashar al-Assad's forces in the Syrian conflict

Conclusion

Left out of the foregoing discussion are the suicide bombings, whether perpetrated by individuals or by death squads, because it is difficult to explore other than superficially any leisure-related motives that might drive such activity. It is probably inspired by an inescapable sense of religious duty, rendering the activity a coercive obligation. That said, some obligations in life can be complex and difficult to meet, with suicide bombings being no exception, it appears. The bomber must be able to make the explosives, conceal them well, know how and where to achieve maximum effect with the explosion, and the like, all aspects of a serious pursuit. These could be interpreted as interesting, challenging, agreeable requirements, even while they help fulfill an ultimately unpleasant duty. Yet, in conclusion, we are still unable to say with any certainty, given the present state of knowledge, whether suicide bombings are leisure or disagreeable obligation.

Then there is kidnapping and hijacking, common motives for which are money and bargaining tokens, sometimes both. The goal is to extract money or other advantage from an individual or a governmental or nongovernmental organization for the benefit of a group, cause, or lone kidnapper. Note that such activity is not necessarily brutal, however; the abducted victims may not be physically harmed. Furthermore, though considerable planning and knowledge are commonly required in such undertakings, they are usually one-shot affairs. To the extent that they are uncoerced, they are thus of the project-based form of leisure. However, a kidnapping, intended to bring significant wealth to the one or a few abductors of an individual believed to have access to the demanded ransom, is best viewed theoretically as a kind of work project. When the goal is to create a bargaining lever and no immediate living is possible from the act, then the event seems best conceived of as a volunteer project, albeit not your run-of-the-mill variety.

Al-bab.com, a spokes-organization for Arab culture, presents a table displaying the "kidnapping events" in Yemen from 1996 to 2001, forty-seven of them all told. Slightly less than half the victims were tourists, with the rest being non-tourists living in Yemen or visiting on business. Al-bab.com says that "virtually every kidnap can be explained in terms of specific grievances. Demands for better local facilities are one common cause; another is the release of prisoners (who may well be regarded as having been 'kidnapped' by the state)." Ben Whitaker (2000) goes on to point out that measures to deter kidnappers fail to remove the grievances behind them. The unequal distribution of national resources is grounds for many of the kidnappings, which will probably to continue until governmental funds are allocated in a way that is both sufficiently transparent and patently fair.[45]

Why do some people in the MENA—and elsewhere for that matter—find brutal leisure so attractive? The answers to this question offered in this chapter are incomplete, necessarily so since its full examination would take us far beyond the scope of our book (e.g., can brutal leisure be explained medically as behavior caused by sadistic personality disorder?). Still, the attraction of brutal leisure can be explained, in part, by the fact that when participating in it, the terrorist, the assassin, and the others realize the six qualities of the serious pursuits (perseverance, effort, knowledge/skill, benefits, ethos, and identity). There is also the seduction of risk, so aptly described by Lyng (1990). We have seen, too, that critical grievances may be motivators for some people, just as religious obligations are for some others. This theme is continued on a broader plane in the next chapter, the first section of which features a discussion of well-being. To the extent it is leisure and not coerced by the likes of sadistic personality disorder, the brutal kind seems capable of generating its own version of this state.

Notes

41. Source: http://www.worldlifeexpectancy.com/cause-of-death/violence/by-country, retrieved 27 November 2011.
42. Source: http://www.nctc.gov/site/technical/index.html, retrieved 12 November 2011.
43. Source: http://www.trutv.com/library/crime/notorious_murders/famous/theo_van_gogh/4.html, retrieved 11 November 2011.
44. Source: http://www.hilalplaza.com/Today-Muslims/Shiite-Shia-Sunni-Conflict.html retrieved 23 November 2011.
45. Source: http://www.al-bab.com/yemen/data/kidnap.htm, retrieved 24 November 2011.

7

Implications for the
Arab/Iranian MENA

This chapter is devoted to three broad contemporary issues arising from chapters 2 through 5, issues that have a special relationship to leisure, work, and community involvement in the MENA. The three issues are personal well-being, community development, and as a celebrated part of the second, democratic advance. All three fall under the heading of cultural development, as defined in chapter 1. So there will be no mistake, remember that cultural development is treated of here as social development, rather than as, for example, development of the economy or of a particular natural resource.

Well-Being

Well-being has been conceptualized both psychologically and sociologically. Edward Diener (2000) defines psychological well-being as a combination of positive affect and general life satisfaction. Corey Keyes' (1998, 121) complementary sociological definition portrays well-being as "the absence of negative conditions and feelings, the result of adjustment and adaptation to a hazardous world." For him well-being, though a personal state, is influenced by many of the social conditions considered earlier and incorporated in the SLP. To put the matter positively, let us say that all well-being comes with having good health, reasonable prosperity, and in general, being routinely happy and content.

And, speaking of being happy, Diener holds that happiness and subjective well-being are the same. Nevertheless, the vestment of happiness is not always cut from the same cloth. Thus happiness is sometimes seen as emerging over a broad swath of life, as expressed in such observations as: "I was happy as a child," "My years in this community have been happy ones," "I will be happy in retirement." This is *long-term happiness* (Stebbins 2011a). It is to be distinguished from *short-term happiness*, or that happiness generated in the present lasting for a few minutes up to a few days. Examples include: "I was happy with my performance on the test," "I am happy that my party turned out so well," "I was very happy to receive that award the other day." Well-being, though increased by fleeting, happy experiences, refers only to a much more enduring personal state and is therefore synonymous only with long-term happiness.

This leads to the following proposition: well-being emanates from a high quality of life, where the latter is founded on one or more serious pursuits reasonably balanced with either casual or project-based leisure activities or a combination of all three forms. In other words, well-being is a central element in an agreeable, possibly even optimal, lifestyle that is anchored in a judicious mix of leisure and work activities. This proposition is useful as a broad precept, but as the next two paragraphs show, the relationships set out in it are actually more complex than meets the eye.

For example, can a serious leisure activity, though not coerced, engender well-being when it is also engenders certain costs and occupies a marginal status with reference to the three social institutions of work, leisure, and family? The answer is, tentatively, yes it can. For, to the extent that well-being is fostered by fulfillment through life's ordinary activities, research evidence suggests that it is an important by-product of serious leisure (Haworth 1986; Haworth and Hill 1992; Mannell 1993). As additional evidence the respondents in my several studies of serious leisure, when interviewed, invariably described in detail and with great enthusiasm the profound fulfillment they derived from their amateur, hobbyist, and volunteer activities.

All this evidence, however, is at bottom only correlational. No one has yet carried out a properly controlled study expressly designed to ascertain whether long-term involvement in a form of serious leisure actually leads to significant and enduring increases in feelings of well-being. The extent to which serious leisure can generate major interpersonal role conflict for some practitioners—it led to two divorces among the twenty-five respondents in a study of amateur theater (Stebbins [1979, 81–83]; on family conflict in running, see Goff, Flick, and Oppliger [1997])—should be warning enough to avoid postulating an automatic link between serious leisure, on the one hand, and well-being, on the other. And, later in this chapter I treat of the effects of selfishness in serious and casual leisure. I also have anecdotal evidence that the serious pursuits can generate intrapersonal conflict, evident when people fail to establish priorities among their many and varied leisure interests or among those interests and their devotee work. This implies that even an approach-approach conflict between cherished leisure/work activities may unfavorably affect well-being. Hamilton-Smith (1995, 6–7) said over fifteen years ago that our lack of knowledge about the link between serious leisure and well-being is a major lacuna in contemporary leisure research. His observation is still current.

Subjective or social, the concept of well-being rests on the presupposition that, to achieve it, people must be proactive, must exercise personal agency to arrive at this state. Well being is therefore also a goal, which when reached will also attest a person's overall happiness. The same may be said for obtaining a decent quality of life. Both concepts speak to a process of personal betterment, as the individual defines this state. Happiness is therefore further explained by our willingness to work toward our own well-being and attractive quality of life.

Although leisure and devotee work are not happiness, they clearly play a pivotal role in generating this state. We should never lose sight of this relationship with one of today's most vibrant spheres of life, for to do so would be to miss an opportunity to promote the relevance of leisure and devotee work to matters that count with science and the general public. Moreover, even if some (mostly casual) leisure leads only to short-term, superficial happiness, it is nonetheless a kind of happiness. Indeed, it is the only kind of happiness that the majority of members in any society ever experience.

In this book, I am trying to show the Arabs and Iranians living in the MENA the many free-time avenues that may be taken to reach the goal of well-being and long-term happiness and the nature of the many benefits that may be found along the way. I am especially plugging the serious pursuits and project-based leisure as the most direct and effective routes to this state, primarily because they are more profound and enduring than casual leisure. In effect, I am arguing that, whereas money is generally a poor currency for buying happiness (Layard 2005, chap. 5), leisure and devotee work offer a much stronger means to this end. The serious pursuits and project-based leisure are far more likely to lead to long-term happiness, especially when, with the casual form, all three are integrated in an OLL.

The personal conditions contributing to well-being and happiness were discussed in chapter 1. The ten rewards presented there, which are available through the serious pursuits, as well as through some leisure projects, number among the main bricks in the foundation of a person's well-being. Psychological flow also fits here. Another important brick is that of self-fulfillment. A fulfilling experience, or more precisely, a set of chronological experiences leads to development to the fullest of a person's gifts and character, to development of that person's full potential. Remember Friedman's observation presented at the beginning of chapter 5 that many Arabs have come to see themselves as deprived of the freedom to develop "anywhere near their full potential." They lack the freedom but, I am saying here, not the opportunity to find self-fulfillment. In fact, Deborah Kapchan (1996) has shown for a sample of Moroccan women that they have found both in the previously all-male domains of the market (suq) and public performance, where they now act as vendors, herbalists, musicians, and marketplace orators.

Career and Life Course

Since well-being is a long-term state, it is also substantially affected by how a person's leisure and work careers and personal life course develop over the years. Unlike a career, linked as it is to a particular role or activity, the life course is much broader, covering numerous roles and activities as they evolve, interweave, and are adopted or abandoned across the lifetime of an individual (modified from Bush and Simmons 1990, 155–157). Furthermore, life course, viewed sociologically, centers on age-graded roles and generational effects. Thus it has a historical dimension, as well as links to social structure based on the status associated with each role. For instance, Fisher, Day, and Collier (1998) observed that old age is uniquely characterized by "generativity," which includes taking on the responsibility of caring for others as carried out through such roles as parent, spouse, friend, and grandparent. When not perceived as personal obligation, such care may lead to fulfillment in a leisure role. Of all the age periods composing the life course, the third age, or that period of life between age fifty and seventy-five (also known as the age of the "young-old" or "active retirement"), offers the richest opportunity for finding fulfillment (Laslett 1994). Brooks (2007) and Wuthnow (2007), by contrast, discuss the still, little-understood "odyssey years," or that period after adolescence and before full adulthood (roughly ages eighteen to thirty-five) during which people in this category commonly exist in a state of uncertainty about matters like marriage, work, education, family, and even leisure. This condition has an impact, sometimes positive, sometimes negative, on well-being.

Given the centrality of familial-tribal organization in much of the MENA, it should be understood that life course is a broader idea than the related one of family life cycle, in that the latter is limited to family concerns. Additionally, although the family life cycle is chronological, as are career and life course, it is not essentially processual. Process is a continuous series of actions, events, and changes, and in the social sciences it includes the assumption that these actions and so on emerge from, or are influenced by, each other in seamless fashion. Moreover, this influence may have past (retrospective), present (immediate), and future (prospective) components. Life cycle, on the other hand, deals with historically arrayed, discrete slices of time, often called phases, and within each, events and actions are typically treated of as static. Rhona and Robert Rapoport (1975) conducted the classic study of leisure and the family life cycle. In short, the life course offers a special slant on leisure, well-being, and social process.

Well-Being as Social Process

The most obvious link between these two is that human social life is, in significant part, processual, and a complete scientific explanation of that life must of necessity include this aspect of it. More subtly, however, is the fact that people's careers and life courses, as processes, are important because they constitute strong motivational forces. Agency is not only a main source of personal action, it is also the process by which the individual carries out that action. Thus, both success and failure in a career in a serious pursuit often motivate people to try to build on the first to achieve still more of it, while doing what they can to avoid the second. Concerning life course, among other things, people often seem to want to harmonize personal interests and the obligations associated with a role or activity. Wearing and Fullagar (1996), for example, concluded from their studies of Australian women that, today, some of them are modifying traditional family roles to put themselves in a position to pursue activities not ordinarily open to females.

Moreover, both career and life course, by dint of their emergent qualities, encourage people to take stock of what has happened up to a certain point in time in a particular career or across one's life as a whole. The "life review" (Butler 1963) said to be common among the elderly, exemplifies stock-taking of the life-course variety. It involves returning to past experiences and unresolved conflicts to make new interpretations of both, the aim being to reintegrate them into life as

155

it has since unfolded. Successful reintegration can bring a sense of well-being, fostered by new positive significance and meaning, to the life course of the subject and prepare this person for death. Likewise, careers in particular roles seem to encourage at numerous junctures both retrospective and prospective reviews of how they have gone and how they will or may go in the future. Strategizing about how to pursue a career in the present or the future is part of this stock-taking, and to the extent that the observations and possibilities are agreeable, this can be a positive process adding thereby yet another brick to the foundation of well-being.

This is as true of leisure roles as it is of the non-leisure kind. Still, this observation is probably most valid for the roles and activities embodying the serious pursuits, where over the long-term, there are skills and knowledge to develop and apply and experience to accumulate and benefit from. The life review in old age could certainly include interpretation of the good and the bad experienced in earlier and present roles and activities in the serious pursuits.

Identity

The sixth distinguishing quality of serious leisure is that its participants tend to identify strongly with their chosen pursuits (see chapter 1). No small wonder. With a formative career in the relevant activity, it is inevitable participants will come to see themselves, usually proudly, as a certain kind of amateur, hobbyist, or career volunteer. True, self-perception as a particular kind of amateur depends on how far into the career the individual has got. Neophytes—serious leisure participants at the beginning of their leisure career but intending to stay with the activity and develop in it—are unlikely to identify themselves as true amateurs or hobbyists. To do that, they must believe they are good enough at it to stand out from its dabblers, even while they are comparatively weak vis-à-vis more experienced participants, including in the case of amateurs, the professionals in their field.

Identity has both a social and a psychological side. Thus a person's identity is part of his personality, which in one sense, is a psychological matter. The individual enthusiast's view of self as an ongoing participant in complex work or leisure activity (serious and project-based forms) is a situated expression of this personal identity. It is based on dimensions like level of skill, knowledge, and experience, as well as number and quality of physical acquisitions (e.g., good health, collectibles) and lasting physical products (e.g., quilts, paintings) stemming from the leisure or work. So, a young woman might remark to a new acquaintance that she is a skateboarder, but qualify the image she is projecting by noting that she has only been in the hobby two years. She is a skateboarder and proud of it, but do not look to her, at least just yet, for expert demonstrations of its core activities. This presentation of self to the acquaintance is a sociological matter, however, in that the skateboarder not only wants the other to know about her leisure but also for that person to form an accurate impression of her ability to partake in it.

A person's social identity refers to the collective view that the other people in a particular leisure or work setting hold of these same levels and acquisitions. It is by social identity, among other ways, that the community (including family, neighbors, and friends) places people in social space. So, John not only sees and identifies himself as a coin collector, but also various members of the community identify him this way. The fact that complex leisure and work offer a distinctive personal and social identity is central to personal development. Moreover, it is a point that leisure educators throughout the world should emphasize. For such an identity is unavailable in casual leisure—the leisure most people know—suggesting, therefore, that the large majority of people receiving leisure education will find the idea a novelty.

The Commonwealth Secretariat (2007) has issued a report extolling the virtues of the "cosmopolitan identities" that people of different nationalities and religions share across these two global, rigid, often fractious social divisions. Cosmopolitan identities, which tend to be positive anchors in life, include being parents, fans of a particular sport, music buffs, kinds of hobbyists, devotees in given occupations, and so on. They surmount the cultural obstacle of fissiparousness/oppositionalism. Such interests can be powerful, overriding in certain situations many other categorical placements, many of them demographic. Thus, Stebbins (1976) found that classical musicians were typically far less concerned about the sex, race, and social class of their partners in the ensemble than about their ability to play their instruments. Concerted music is no fun to play—this leisure is spoiled—when a key player performs it poorly. We will return to this idea in the next chapter, where we consider the possibilities of leisure and community involvement in the MENA serving as two main avenues to cultural development.

Community Development

My stance in this section is that cultural development creates fertile soil for community development. In chapter 1 we defined community involvement as local voluntary action, where members of a local community participate together in nonprofit groups or in other community activities. My argument in the present chapter is threefold: (1) In satisfying their desire for leisure or work, many people are drawn to community involvement. (2) The fulfillment and enjoyment they find there in mingling with other members of the community motivates many of those same people to continue with these social activities. (This argument is set out in greater detail in Stebbins [2002].) (3) Furthermore, community involvement helps cut down the cultural obstacle of corporate weakness.

It was observed previously that citizen participation, which has a decidedly political hue, is but one type of community involvement. It is conceived of scientifically as a mechanism for accomplishing the democratic goals of a society or organization. This conception is much in vogue today in the West, while its applicability in the MENA was called into question in the preceding chapter. Notwithstanding that pessimistic statement, citizen participation will come in for considerable discussion in this the final section of the present chapter.

By contrast, the much broader idea of community involvement denotes individual participation by any member of the community, whether officially a citizen, in any local, collective, uncoerced activity. The implication in this broad conception is that such participation helps in some significant way to sustain the community of which the participant is a member. Whereas this way may be political (e.g., working for a political party, working to change a local bylaw), it is more likely to be nonpolitical, as in volunteering for a local charity or coaching a youth sports team. The fact is that both *political* citizen participation and *community* involvement help sustain the local community, primarily by enabling its members, as citizens, friends, neighbors, relatives, and workmates, to associate with one another along the lines of all manner of shared interests. A community is, among other things, a large social group in which members interact with one another (even if all members lack direct contact with all other members), such that this group develops a distinctive identity and, by dint of such participation, continues to flourish as a collectivity.

Community Involvement as Leisure

In chapter 1 we distinguished community involvement and leisure. To obviate confusion, the distinction—it is subtle but important—bears repeating. Leisure, to the extent it is social, done with, or oriented toward one or more other people, is a pivotal kind of community involvement. This is perhaps most obvious for the leisure that is undertaken as volunteering, the altruistic intent of which is to improve community life in some particular way. Other kinds of leisure, however, though also instances of community involvement, are usually not pursued expressly to improve social life. In other words, the amateur and hobbyist pursuits are primarily inspired by self-interest, but when collective, have altruistic overtones. It is the opposite for volunteering, where altruism dominates and self-interest is less central (Stebbins 1982). Self-interest reigns supreme for all casual leisure, save the volunteering type; here the driving force is to find a certain kind of hedonic pleasure.

Much of what I have written in the past under this heading has borne on the contributions made by serious leisure enthusiasts to the social and cultural enrichment of their local community (reviewed in Stebbins [2001a] and Stebbins [2007a]). This kind of community involvement is evident when, for example, every three or four months the town's civic orchestra provides it with a concert of classical music or the local astronomy society offers an annual "star night," during which the public may observe the heavens using the telescopes of club members. And model railroaders in the area sometimes mount exhibitions of the fruits of their hobby for popular consumption. Lyons and Dionigi (2007) found, in a study of older Australian adults in the Masters sports (sports competitions for seniors), that, through their participation there, they feel a sense of "giving something back" to the community. Though most thinkers in the area fail to conceive of these activities as voluntary action, they certainly fit the definition of such action, as do the activities discussed in the next paragraph. Furthermore Hemmingway (1999) and Reid (1995) have argued that, when considering leisure's contribution to community, it is important to distinguish between different kinds of activities. The examples above—all of them serious leisure—illustrate contributions quite distinct from those made through the casual or project-based forms.

A somewhat broader sort of community involvement (sometimes also carried out on a regional or societal level) springs from the pursuit of volunteer activities, which may be enacted as serious, casual, or project-based leisure. This is, indeed, the most common conception of community involvement, which is sometimes discussed as "civil labor." It, too, is voluntary action, although a type that finds members of a local community participating together as volunteers in nonprofit groups and other community activities. On this level, a principal intention is to improve community life. Civil labor differs from community involvement mainly in emphasis; it is on human activity devoted to unpaid renewal and expansion of social capital (Rojek 2002, 21). Beck (2000, 125) holds that civil labor comprises housework, family work, club work, and volunteer work. This is an extremely general conception, however, since it includes the area of unpaid work, a major part of which can be qualified as disagreeable nonwork obligation.

For Rojek (2002, 26–27), however, civil labor consists mainly of the community contributions of amateurs, hobbyists, and career volunteers made when they pursue their serious leisure. This is precisely what Leadbeater and Miller (2004) have in mind in their treatise about how amateurs in various fields are shaping the twentieth-first century economy and society in the West. Helft (2007) offers a concrete example in an article about amateur mapmakers, who using simple Internet tools, are reshaping online map services and offering viewers far more detail of many more geographic sites than heretofore available. Along these same lines Levine (2007) writes that democracy depends on citizen participation, and too many of today's young Americans lack the skills needed for this.

Civil labor, however conceived of, generates "social capital," defined here, following Putnam (2000, 19), as the links among individuals manifested in social networks, trustworthiness, acts motivated by the norm of reciprocity, and the like that develop in a community or larger society. The idea was created as an analogy to the concepts of human capital and physical capital (e.g., financial resources, natural resources); it emphasizes that human groups of all kinds also benefit from and advance their interests according to the salutary interrelations of their members. Community involvement also generates social capital, but as noted earlier, it includes amateur and hobbyist activities; as just observed, this result, though it occurs, is not the primary reason for pursuing them.

With one exception to be discussed shortly, casual leisure appears not to make this kind of contribution to community. True, people are sometimes joined in such leisure with strangers, especially these days, over the Internet. The same happens with tribes: fragmented groupings left over from the preceding era of mass consumption, groupings recognized today by their unique tastes, lifestyles, and form of social organization (Maffesoli 1996). Maffesoli identifies and describes this postmodern phenomenon, which spans national borders. In this regard, he observes that mass culture has disintegrated, leaving in its wake a diversity of tribes, including the followers of heavy metal music and those youth who participate in raves. Tribes are special leisure organizations, special ways of organizing the pursuit of particular kinds of casual leisure. Tribes are also found in serious leisure, but not, however, in project-based leisure (see Stebbins [2002, 69–71]). Tribes, social worlds, casual leisure, and serious leisure are related in Figure 7.1.

Figure 7.1
Structural Complexity: From Tribes to Social Worlds

Taste-based tribes (e.g., music, clothing)	Activity-based tribes: consumers (e.g., jazz, basketball)	Activity-based tribes: buffs (e.g., soap opera)	SocialWorlds of (e.g., amateurs, career volunteers)
least			most

→   →   →

complex   complex

Casual leisure	Casual leisure	Serious leisure	Serious leisure

From: Stebbins, R.A. (2002). *The organizational basis of leisure participation: A motivational exploration.* State College, PA: Venture, p. 70.

But, in the taste- and activity-based tribal casual leisure mentioned in Figure 7.1, scant contribution is made to the community. I have also excluded from this discussion of community involvement the type of casual leisure observed in regular sessions of sociable conversation among friends or acquaintances, for example, in the hookah bar, with other men or women in the suq, and during the friendly gathering after weekly religious services. To be sure, these sessions are both social and voluntary, but they are not, however, altruistic voluntary action. It follows that they are neither civil labor nor sources of social capital.

This, as I stated earlier, is also true of nearly all other casual leisure, the glaring exception being casual volunteering; it being done expressly as civil labor. And, in the course of doing it, volunteers may well meet and serve with people never before encountered. So we must conclude, contrary to Rojek, that such labor is not limited to serious leisure, but also finds its place in the volunteer type of casual leisure.

Moreover, volunteer project-based leisure may be conceived of as civil labor. Project-based leisure has potential in at least two ways for building community. First, it too can bring into contact people who otherwise have no reason to meet, or at least meet frequently. Second, by way of event volunteering and other short-term, collective altruistic activity, it can contribute to carrying off community events and projects. In other words some project-based leisure (mostly one-shot volunteer projects, it appears) can also be understood as civil labor, as just defined, suggesting further that such activity can be other than serious leisure. In fact, the mountain hobbyists studied by the author (Stebbins 2005a) occasionally rounded out their leisure lifestyles by sporadically undertaking or participating in projects (typically volunteer) of this nature.

Clearly, to be community involvement, leisure must be collective in some fashion; the reclusive hobbies (among them, the liberal arts, some amateur piano and guitar), for example, fail to qualify. Furthermore, when it comes to social capital, as opposed to civil labor and community involvement, I do not believe a case exists for privileging any of the three forms of leisure as the principal or most important way of generating the former. What is important is that people come together in voluntary action, as motivated by voluntary altruism, doing so long enough to, for example, learn something beyond stereotype about one another, learn to trust one another (hopefully only where experience warrants), develop "other-regarding" or altruistic love for one another (Jeffries et al. 2006), and for these reasons become willing to continue their interaction. Many forms of serious leisure encourage sustained contact capable of fostering such learning, as seen in routine participation in many volunteer emergency services, hobbyist clubs, and arts and sports groups. Project-based leisure can also be a source of social capital, though here, such capital is of more limited scope than that generated through enduring serious leisure activities. As for casual leisure volunteering, it may be short- or long-term.

Selfishness

It would be reasonable to ask why I have included a section on something as negative as selfishness in a book bearing substantially on leisure, which is the very foundation of the positive side of human social life (Stebbins 2009b). The answer is, in part, that I believe in presenting a balanced picture of the idea of community involvement. For "community involvement" has become, for many people, one of those warm-and-fuzzy ideas that sends shivers of virtue, kindliness, and compassion up and down the spine. Not surprising, since a similar sentimental *frisson* is also felt in the same circles when the word "community" enters the conversation. Both concepts, in the least discerning of conceptualizations, constitute an unalloyed good. Nevertheless, selfishness sometimes clothes these ordinarily positive aspects of life in dark apparel, especially as experienced by the people who are victims of it. Yet, viewed through the lens of community involvement, selfishness may also have positive consequences.

Selfishness is the act of a self-seeker judged as selfish by the victim of that act (Stebbins 1981). When we define an act as selfish, we make an imputation. This imputation is most commonly hurled at perceived self-seekers by their victims, where the self-seekers are felt to demonstrate a concern for their own welfare or advantage at the expense of or in disregard for those victims. The central thread running through the fabric of selfishness is exploitative unfairness—a kind of personal favoritism infecting the everyday affairs of many people in modern society. What is exploitative and unfair is, of course, to be interpreted in the MENA according to local norms.

In comparing the three forms, it is evident that the serious pursuits are nearly always the most complicated and enduring of them and, for this reason, often take up much more of a participant's time (Stebbins 1995). They are therefore much more likely to generate charges of selfishness. For instance some types of serious, and even some project-based, leisure can only be pursued according to a rigid schedule (e.g., amateur theatrical rehearsals, volunteer guide work at a zoo, volunteer ticket selling at an arts festival), which unlike most casual leisure, allows little room for compromise or maneuver. Thus imputations of selfishness are considerably more likely to arise with regard to the first two.

Furthermore, we can make a similar observation about serious and causal leisure activities that exclude the participant's partner vis-à-vis those that include this person. Logically speaking, it is difficult to complain about someone's selfishness when the would-be complainer also engages in the activity, especially with significant fulfillment. Furthermore, serious leisure, compared with casual leisure, is often more debatable as selfishness, when seen from the standpoints of both the victim and the self-seeker. For serious leisure enthusiasts have at their fingertips as justifications for their actions such venerated ideals as self-enrichment, self-expression, self-actualization, service to others, contribution to group effort, development of a valued personal identity, and the regeneration of oneself after work. As for casual volunteering, it

163

is a partial exception to this observation, in that it, too, can be justified, though only by some of these ideals. They are, most notably, volunteer service to others and personal regeneration.

I have argued elsewhere (Stebbins 2007a, 75) that selfishness is part of the culture of leisure, a proposition based on my observations over the years that many participants in all three forms share a tendency to act in this way. Moreover this tendency and the problems it can engender appear to be fully recognized in leisure circles, though admittedly, the matter has yet to be formally studied. Selfishness roots, to some extent, in the uncontrollability of leisure activities. They engender in participants the desire to engage in them beyond the time or the money (if not both) available for free-time interests. That is leisure enthusiasts are often eager to spend more time at and money on the core activity than is likely to be countenanced by certain important others who also makes demands on that time and money. The latter may conclude, sooner or later, that the enthusiast is more enamored of the core leisure activity than of, say, the partner or spouse. When a participant, seemingly out of control, takes on too much of the activity, imputations of selfishness (whether overtly made or covertly held) from certain important others is surely just around the corner. This is the negative side of selfishness and its impact on positive relationships and small groups (e.g., families, friendship groups).

What, then, is the positive side? The answer, in brief, is that, as argued earlier in this chapter, serious leisure, even when selfish, is still community involvement. And such involvement helps generate social capital. But do these lofty ends (e.g., providing the community with amateur theater, volunteering in a local Rotary club project, volunteer work for the Pan Arab Games) justify the selfish means by which they are sometimes reached? Do the ends justify either exploitative selfishness or other contentious practices along the way? More broadly we must never fail to also consider the moral dimension of community involvement.

The Organization of Leisure

Djaït (2011, 139) observes that, for democracy to succeed in the MENA, there must be organization, and the cities are the main centers for its development. Specifically, most community involvement in the MENA, as elsewhere, is carried out by way of one or more kinds of social organization (defined shortly). In leisure, as in most other areas of life, many activities are structured, or organized, in small groups, social networks, and grassroots organizations, as well as in larger complex organizations and still more broadly, in tribes (considered in the previous section), social worlds, and social movements (Stebbins 2002). Each structures the social behavior of its members in particular ways, some of those ways being unique to that kind of organization. And, as stated earlier, individual interests also structure the organizational entities that facilitate these interests, which includes establishing those entities in the first place. Here the positive role of human agency is again evident. Thus we may say about leisure organizations, as with other kinds of organizations, that participation in them amounts to a two-way street of influence, running from individual to collectivity and the reverse. This is the first of three critical assumptions on which this discussion of leisure and organization is based.

The second critical assumption is that members of the different sorts of organizations (defined below in the wide sense of social organization) know they are members. Third, such people value highly their membership, for given that we are considering only leisure organizations entered without coercion, members would abandon them were they substantially disvalued. Moreover, when they are highly valued, belonging itself becomes an important motive, since membership enables pursuit of one or more of the leisure activities the organization promotes and facilitates, and its members are eager to pursue. In other words, belonging to a leisure organization adds to one's sense of well-being. Yet it should be clear that belonging to any of these organizational entities, even when centered on leisure, is never wholly a positive experience; for example, spouses have their tiffs, dissension shakes up some groups, ideological tensions can splinter a social movement, and so on.

Let us note before going further into the matter of the organization of leisure that many leisure activities in all three forms also appear to allow for, if not require, solitary participation, volunteering being the chief exception. Thus, someone may, in solitude, play the piano or the guitar, collect rocks or seashells, sit and daydream, or assemble a complicated electronic device from a kit. Volunteering, however, is inherently organizational in the broad sense of the word, since by definition, it involves directly or indirectly serving other people, be they individuals or groups. What, then, do I mean by "the broad sense" of the concept of organization?

Organization is used here as shorthand for the range of collectivities mentioned at the start of this section (dyads to social movements) that add social and psychological structure to leisure life. Accordingly, discussion in this section will center primarily on these different types manifested as leisure organizations rather than on the community or societal organization of leisure, as seen in the sweeping communal arrangements that make available leisure services and opportunities. Additionally the present book requires only an aperçu of the different kinds of organization common in leisure, with a fuller treatment of them being available elsewhere (Stebbins 2002).

Let us begin, then, by noting that some leisure is pursued in dyads (e.g. two friends organizing a surprise birthday party for someone or going together to the cinema). The triad is another recognizable arrangement within which to partake of leisure (e.g., three people on a fishing trip, a classical music trio). Dyads and triads are the smallest of the human small groups, which theoretically run to around twenty members (Stebbins 2002, chap. 2). Examples of leisure in the larger small groups include the community soccer team, several friends who routinely hike together, and a group of people who routinely participate in a book club. These three types of organization are found in all three forms of leisure.

Turning to the social network, the definition that best fits the small amount of work done on this form of organization within the domain of leisure is Elizabeth Bott's (1957, 59). Hers is simple: a social network is "a set of social relationships for which there is no common boundary." In the strict sense of the word, a network is not a structure, since it has no shared boundaries (boundaries recognized by everyone in the structure), no commonly recognized hierarchy, and no central coordinating agency. Nevertheless, links exist between others in the network, in that some members are directly in touch with each other, while other members are not. That is, we find here a measure of social organization.

As individuals pursue their leisure interests, they commonly develop networks of friends and acquaintances related in one way or another to these interests. When a person acquires more such interests, the number of networks tends to grow accordingly, bearing in mind, however, that members of some of these will sometimes overlap. For instance, a few members of Mohammed's falcon breeding network—they might be suppliers, veterinarians, or other breeders—are also members of his golf network—who might be suppliers, course personnel, or other golfers. Knowing about people's leisure networks helps explain how they, through positive agency, socially allocate their free time. In this manner, as Blackshaw and Long (1998, 246) pointed out, we learn something new about leisure lifestyle.

At the next level of organization—the grassroots association—serious leisure predominates, though some manifestations of it can also be found in casual leisure. As for project-based leisure, its very nature would seem to discourage grassroots associations from emerging around this form. According to Smith (2000, 8):

> grassroots associations are locally based, significantly autonomous, volunteer-run formal nonprofit (i.e., voluntary) groups that manifest substantial voluntary altruism as groups and use the associational form of organization and, thus, have official memberships of volunteers who perform most, and often all, of the work/activity done in and by these nonprofits.

The term "formal" in this definition refers in fact to a scale of structure and operations that, in an actual association, may be informal, semiformal, or formal. Moreover, the line separating grassroots associations from paid-staff voluntary groups—treated in the next paragraph as volunteer organizations—is unavoidably fuzzy, distinguishing the two being primarily a matter of gradation. Both types fall under the heading of voluntary groups: "nonprofit groups of any type, whether grassroots associations or based on paid staff, and whether local, national, or international in scope" (Smith 2000, ix). In harmony with this statement, we may say that some of the groups listed in the preceding paragraphs (e.g., the community soccer team) are also grassroots associations, as are such formal entities as Scout troops, stamp collectors' societies, hikers' clubs, abused women's shelters, and the Islamic *Qurbani Waqf*, which provides meat to the needy.

By comparison, volunteer organizations offer leisure only to career and casual volunteers and to volunteers serving on projects. Volunteer organizations are distinguished by their reliance on paid staff, and by the fact that they are established to facilitate work for a cause or provision of a service rather than pursuit of a pastime. They nonetheless depend significantly on volunteer help to reach their objectives.

Pearce (1993, 15), writing about Britain and more generally the West, holds that by far the largest number of volunteers work in these organizations (whether this generalization holds for the MENA remains to be established). Yet some volunteer organizations may be staffed entirely by remunerated employees, volunteers only being engaged as unpaid members of their boards of directors. Hospitals

167

and universities present two main examples. Many of the foundations may be similarly classified. Other volunteer organizations have a more even mix of paid and volunteer personnel; they include Greenpeace, Amnesty International, and the Red Cross. Finally, some have only one or two employees, with all other work being conducted by volunteers. They are, at bottom, grassroots associations that have grown complicated enough to justify paying someone to help with certain of the group's routine operations that its volunteers are unable or unwilling to carry out.

Leisure service organizations are not voluntary groups, as just defined. Rather, they are collectivities consisting of a paid staff who provide one of more leisure services to a targeted clientele. To be sure, the clients are engaging in particular leisure activities, but the organizations providing them are not themselves leisure organizations as described in this section. Leisure service organizations are established either to make a profit (the goal of many a health spa, amusement park, and the various language schools, for example) or in some instances, to simply make enough money to continue offering their services. This latter goal motivates charitable, nonprofit groups like Jordan's Family Reconciliation House (see chapter 5), the YMCA and YWCA, and the adult education program as well as the governmental leisure and recreational programs and services.

The next two types of organization germane to leisure have already been considered: social worlds were described in chapter 1, and tribes were covered earlier in this chapter. Let me now add that the richest development of social worlds may be observed in serious leisure, and if found at all in casual and project-based leisure, they are, by comparison, much simpler in composition. Refer to Figure 7.1 for a schematic view of the interrelationship of these two types of organization with casual and serious leisure.

What remains, then, to be examined in this section on leisure and organization is the social movement. A social movement is a noninstitutionalized set of networks, small groups, and formal organizations that, having coalesced around a significant value, inspires members to promote or resist change with reference to that value. The first question is whether participation in a social movement is a leisure activity. The answer is both yes and no, for it depends on the movement in question. Movements abound that gain members through their own volition, suggesting that the members experience no significant coercion to become involved. Some religious movements serve as examples, as do movements centered on values like physical fitness and healthy eating. Still, the latter two also include people who feel pressured by outside forces to participate, as when a physician prescribes exercise and weight loss or face an early death. Thus some social movements are composed of enthusiasts who are there for leisure reasons and other people who are compelled to be there (not leisure). Finally, there are movements that seem to find their impetus primarily in people who feel driven to champion a particular cause, such as the women's movement in the MENA, the celebrated temperance movement of early last century, and the vigorous antismoking movement now clamoring for legislative change in many parts of the modern world. Here, a strong sense of obligation fuels participation.

Inside the MENA, the Arab Spring is today's most visible social movement, albeit one that seems cut from mostly obligatory cloth. Still, whether such activity is truly leisure or nonwork obligation will have to be determined empirically through direct research on the motivation of its champions.

Democracy

Theodore Parker, an American clergyman, is said to have observed in a speech in 1850 that "a democracy . . . is a government of all the people, by all the people, for all the people."[46] Daniel Webster, an American statesman, expressed a similar idea twenty years earlier when, in a speech, he spoke of "the people's government, made for the people, made by the people, and answerable to the people."[47] Somewhat later Abraham Lincoln, a mid-nineteenth-century president of the United States, made use of the phraseology in 1863 in his celebrated Gettysburg Address.

Defining democracy in these terms provides a clear link to citizen participation, as conveyed through the words "by the people" (agency, political activities) and "for the people" (goals of political activities). Citizen participation in democracies is not, however, always leisure. Though I have never seen any research on the practice, voting could well be conceived of as a mildly disagreeable obligation, a citizen's nonwork duty. And, whereas some people working for a political party, governmental voting system, or democratic support group (e.g., one encouraging voter turnout or equality in political campaign funding) may feel similarly obligated, most appear to participate in such activities as volunteers, as a leisure pursuit.

Three Principles of Democracy

Parker's pithy dictum, handy as it is for linking citizen participation with democratic procedure, nevertheless ignores certain thorny aspects of that procedure. For this form of government rests on the principles of tolerance, compromise, and leniency. Modern democracies of all levels of development and effectiveness struggle with them. But for incipient democracies these principles pose particularly difficult challenges.

Tolerance is an attitude that we hold toward certain activities or thoughts of others that differ substantially from our own (Stebbins 1996a, 3). It is a relatively passive disposition, falling roughly midway between scorn and disdain toward an activity or thought pattern, on the one hand, and embracement or acceptance of it on the other. Both scorn and embracement are active approaches to the behavior in question. When something is tolerated, we accord it legitimacy, though perhaps grudgingly so. We see it as having a level of threat low enough to refrain from actively opposing it. At the same time, we have little interest in actually adopting the tolerated behaviors or thoughts as our own, or accepting any of them as an alternative we might adopt in the future.

Clearly, if the large majority of people in a heterogeneous society (one having significant social divisions) are intolerant, then democracy is impossible. With this attitude, all the people cannot govern, and all the people will then be unable to benefit from the ensuing intolerant governance. Under this condition only some people—those who have the greatest power and influence—get their way and thereby reach their political goals. Why this outcome?

Intolerance subverts democracy because, among other reasons, it breeds a lack of will to compromise. Compromising is the intermediate way between conflicting requirements or courses of action. It involves mutual concessions by all parties, such that a *modus vivendi* is obtained. No one gets everything he wants, but no one loses totally either. Compromises, like the tolerance on which they are to some extent founded, may well be accepted on the personal level with a measure of bitterness. But some parties to the compromise seem to see it in the broader, positive light of democratic functioning: it is necessary for the greater good, for the continuation of the larger society.

Leniency is also a product of tolerance. In being lenient, we are not, in general, disposed to severity. In particular, leniency manifests itself in the ways we handle deviance in society. At the formal level, the level of law and regulation, it is expressed in codes of conduct and penalties for deviating from them. In a proper democracy, these codes are created by the people for the people, where they determine which punishments fit which crimes. And in a proper democracy, the codes are administered impartially. At the informal level—the level of social control through gossip, discrimination, reprimand, and the like—leniency is expressed in sympathetic but firm language, often an exercise in tough love.

Rampant intolerance in a society will fail to generate leniency on a sufficiently broad scale. Furthermore, those members of it who are threatened by or are victims of what they define as severe, non-lenient treatment (formal or informal) will feel they have been unjustly done by, undemocratically handled with respect to their contentious behavior or thought. Isolated instances of severity are to be expected in democratic systems, which are too complicated to be perfected, but lack of leniency toward one or more of the main social divisions in a society will surely undermine the democratic functioning of the latter. The cultural obstacle of fissiparousness/oppositionalism is founded on intolerance, lack of compromise, and non-leniency, and this, in turn, justifies state dominance by the preponderant divisions.

Selfishness and Moral Standards

A refusal to compromise on issues of political (i.e., democratic) concern in one's country may be interpreted as an instance of selfishness, as exploitation of fellow countrymen for personal gain at the expense of those citizens. Thus, a street evangelist in Calgary, Canada, the author's city of residence, refused to lower the volume of his nightly outdoor broadcasts, even though residents in the area complained (to the city council) that the broadcasts were loud enough to seriously disturb their peace of mind. After a lengthy political battle, the man eventually agreed to reduce substantially the decibels of his amplified messages. A democratic compromise had been struck. In line with this scope of this book, it may be presumed that the man was engaging in one of the core activities of his serious pursuit, namely, that of preacher.

Selfishness is hardly limited to the world of leisure pursuits, but rather also abounds in work and nonwork obligation. Moreover, other morally questionable attitudes, among them greed, stinginess, unkindness, and unfairness, seem to be far more prevalent in these other two domains than in leisure. Expressed in work and nonwork obligation these questionable attitudes are also capable of undermining democracy, primarily by poisoning either the spirit of compromise or that of leniency, if not both. One significant point about this quartet of moral aberrations is their marginal relationship to leisure.

Leisure and Devotee Work as Democracy's Best Friend

The preceding section suggests that democracy is best served—initiated, sustained, improved—through the leisure and devotee work domains of life, as opposed to those of non-devotee work and nonwork obligation. This proposition is based on two others: (1) that moral weakness, as exemplified above, is a main enemy of democracy, and (2) that leisure is democracy's best friend because, when compared with the other two, it harbors notably fewer enemies of this sort. Let us examine these assertions more closely.

Leisure and devotee work, as has been stated throughout, are intrinsically rewarding activity; people pursue free-time activities for the positive experience of engaging in them. True, sometimes amateur athletes, for example, cheat at their sport (unfairness), and as altruistic as they generally are, volunteers occasionally act unkindly toward their targets of benefit. Greed is evident in some areas of casual leisure, such as when a customer buys all the chocolates on sale, thereby leaving none for other bargain hunters. Then there is deviant leisure, with its diverse rejections of society's moral norms. Add to these dark actions the instances of selfishness discussed earlier and it may be concluded that leisure is not a morally pure sphere of life.

Nevertheless, its fundamentally appealing nature appears to protect leisure and devotee work from the notably greater rates of moral turpitude found in the domains of non-devotee work and nonwork obligation. Activities in the latter two are predominantly, if not exclusively, extrinsically motivated (remember that intrinsically motivated devotee work is a serious pursuit). Here, for some people, immoral means can justify their extrinsic ends. But, when the end is intrinsic—found in the activity itself—the means to that end are morally harmonious with it. No need here to try to embellish this experience by cheating or being unkind, for example. Such practices undermine the positiveness of the leisure-devotee work experience being sought. Thus, Delattre (1975) writes that, logically, a person must either cheat at a game or compete in it; it is logically impossible to do both, for competition is the very essence of games. Moreover, when people violate the rules governing competition, they treat their opponents as mere extrinsic means to their end of victory.

As for selfishness, enthusiasts behave this way to enjoy more of their activity. This is certainly a moral issue, but one resting squarely on the intrinsic appeal of that activity. Selfishness follows logically from an exceptional level of intrinsic motivation to engage in the pursuit. By the way, such harmony of motives makes it more difficult for victims to defend their position on the matter.

So, while morally questionable behavior at non-devotee work and in nonwork obligation can undermine democracy, leisure and devotee-work, with their appreciably lower moral baggage, generally can support it. This it does by the mechanisms already considered: civil labor, generating social capital, community involvement, and collective leisure and devotee work pursuits. These mechanisms are active on a broad plane, only a relatively small corner of which is citizen participation constituting the direct link between leisure and democracy. Beyond this specialized field of volunteering, participants in collective leisure of all sorts, but particularly those in the serious pursuits, form ties through these activities with other members of the community and the larger society. Here, to the extent they do this, they help to either break down or circumvent the socially divisive, fissiparous barriers that hinder democratic development.

Conclusions

It is widely understood that the Arab Spring is, in substantial part, about establishing some form of democratic rule in those countries of the MENA touched by the uprisings. The uprisings are based on many grievances, including poverty, unemployment, lack of political expression, gender discrimination, and crucially for this book, insufficient opportunities for human cultural development. Democracy is widely seen among the insurgents as the means for tempering, if not eliminating, this litany of complaints. Yet, the foregoing list of moral weaknesses present, when combined with the fissiparousness and oppositionalism of Arab/Iranian society, a formidable barrier to the envisioned governmental changes. Additionally, the incumbent totalitarian regimes, enjoying state dominance as they do, are so far resisting, tooth and nail, the most profound democratic transformations.

On top of all this Djaït (2011) points out that, as Arabs break with the state, the radical Islam of today is playing on their sensibilities.

173

In fact, in the Arab world the state no longer manages to fulfill its obligations.... A fundamental break has formed between the state and the population.... The population has begun to live on the fringe of the state and, in order to do this, has restored all the forms of solidarity and basic human organization called forth from the past and adapted to present circumstances. It is on these deep, autonomous chords that radical Islamism is playing, guiding people's sensibilities into a world that is adrift, coming to place itself between the inexistent state and a humanity that is on the near side of religion, a humanity of a primary order. (156–157)

To opt for democracy, according to this sacred message, is to reject Arab and (I add) Iranian tradition and risk falling into the abyss of Western modernism.

It is against this black scenario that much of the insurgent MENA is struggling to realize its own cultural development. Leisure, especially the serious pursuits, has a major supporting, if not leading, role to play in this historic drama. But it is no panacea.

Notes

46.   Source: http://www.bartleby.com/100/459.4.html, retrieved 22 September 2011.
47.   Source: http://www.bartleby.com/100/358.html, retrieved 22 September 2011.

Thus chapter 2 contained a section on devotee work and its origins in related serious leisure activities. As far as we know, enthusiasts in these activities do not usually enter them in hope of subsequently finding remunerative work there, with student amateurs and hobbyists being the main exception to this generalization. But, once well-immersed in a kind of serious leisure, participants learn about or discover for themselves how they might make some money in it, whether as a supplement to their livelihood gained elsewhere or as their principal livelihood. The large majority of amateurs and hobbyists I have interviewed over the years wanted nothing to do with this kind of leisure career change. But, then, they were not facing the employment problems that many modern Arabs and Iranians do.

Among the three forms of serious leisure, volunteering has been the area of free-time activities most amenable to occupational experimentation and exploration. Indeed, discussions of "marginal volunteering" revolve, in part, around participants who volunteer expressly to find agreeable remunerative work (Stebbins 2001b). The unemployed and those employed in unpleasant jobs in the MENA might want to try this approach, working from the list of areas of volunteering set out late in chapter 5. Note, however, that using a volunteer activity as a springboard to a paying job does not necessarily mean that the second will be a paid counterpart of the first. In other words, while volunteering, people may discover related kinds of work that are interesting, accessible, and have openings. Volunteers aspiring for these jobs may, by dint of their volunteering experience, be qualified to fill such positions. Alternatively, they may have to seek further training to become qualified.

Unemployment

Unemployment is by no means only about leisure. This is because unemployment does not automatically result in leisure for its victims; for them it automatically results only in time away from work and not in time away from other obligations. Viewed from a different angle, unemployment forces unemployed people into the domain of nonwork obligation, where they feel pressured to find a paying job. This situation is similar to that of boredom, which is in fact a common accompaniment of being unemployed. As such it has raised in social science circles the question of whether a person in such circumstances can find stimulating or true leisure of any kind, be it casual, serious, or project-based.

What evidence exists on the matter suggests that the experience of unemployment varies from person to person and according to the sorts of activities each turns to when trying to counteract its worst effects (Haworth 1986, 288). Still, compared with the unemployed in the lower-level occupations, those in the upper-level occupations, including professionals, are more likely to turn to serious leisure and in this manner ride out the dispiriting effects of their unfortunate economic situation. The former are more often overwhelmed by the act of being thrown out of work, suffering from depression and lethargy to a degree that makes it next to impossible to pursue leisure of any kind (Kay 1990, 415). Part of the problem, it seems, is that they feel useless and browbeaten by social convention to search unceasingly for work, a frame of mind that virtually alienates them from true leisure. That is, they are too demoralized to engage in leisure, it being a purposive activity intended to achieve a particular end. Meanwhile, sitting around idle is neither leisure nor work.

Boas Shamir (1985), in a study of unemployed Israeli men and women with university degrees, found that those with a strong Protestant ethic and prior work involvement were much more likely to turn to, and benefit from, leisure activities than those with a weaker ethic. Tess Kay (1990) studied a small, racially mixed subsample of men and women in Britain who, while unemployed, had developed a sustained interest in certain serious leisure activities. She concluded that, for them, the experience of unemployment had its positive side, whereas for the majority of unemployed people in her main sample, the experience was mostly negative. Lobo and Watkins (1994) obtained similar results in Australia, as did Haworth and Drucker (1991) in Britain.

Based on their exploratory research on caregivers, Weinblatt and Navon (1995) hypothesized that, in certain situations, people actually try to avoid leisure, feeling that they have no right to it because, for example, it is self-interested, prevents meeting serious obligations, and compared with them, is trivial. The unemployed give similar reasons for abstaining from leisure. Thus the "flight from leisure" by them and by Weinblatt and Navon's caregivers raises some difficult questions for the unemployed in the MENA. First of all, do unemployed Arabs and Iranians feel this way? A subsidiary question is, à la Shamir, whether there is an equivalent of the Protestant ethic at work among them. (Shamir [1985] found an equivalent in his Jewish sample.) Second, if they do feel that they must avoid leisure, should we be trying to promote it to them as a main avenue to well-being? Third, can serious leisure and possibly project-based leisure engender well-being under these conditions, after the unemployed in the MENA are made aware of it and become willing to try it?

My answer to the second question has always been no (e.g., Stebbins [1998, 18]). That is, in promoting leisure, we must avoid any sense of coercing people to engage in it. As for the other two questions, we will only know the answers after careful research, conducted both inside and outside the MENA. True, serious leisure is anything but trivial, but it is also self-interested, and given its magnetic appeal and the temptations of selfishness, it could therefore interfere with meeting obligations. Alternatively, undertaking a leisure project from time to time might be, for some, a more realistic, albeit partial, adaptation to the unhappy state of being unemployed.

Serious Leisure as a Substitute for Work

Yet, the displeasure with being unemployed seems to diminish as unemployed people grow accustomed to their situation. In long-term unemployment many former workers, discouraged with the results of their routine search for a job, eventually abandon the search. What they do for their livelihood in these circumstances is complicated and beyond the scope of this book, except however, for the part that serious leisure can play.

To start, we must return to the concept of social world introduced in chapter 2, the set of characteristic groups, events, routines, practices, and organizations, which is held together, to an important degree, by semiformal, or mediated, communication. The social world is not only a concept well in tune with the work and leisure routines of the present and the future; it is also a desideratum of many a modern man and woman both for today and for the years to come. I believe that this holds as well for those in the MENA and for those who are retired wherever they live in this world. If people can no longer find a work organization to belong to or can only belong marginally to one as an outside consultant or part-time employee how, then, can they become part of the community, whether conceived of locally, regionally, nationally, or internationally?

Increasingly, it appears that the only available communal connections for most people will come through activities taking place in their after-work time, even when they have work. Yet, because they tend to be private, purely family activities rarely generate such connections. But those who once found meaningful organizational ties at work can still turn to serious leisure, where one of the principal attractions of most of the amateur, hobbyist, and volunteer activities is the sense of being part of a bustling, fascinating, all-encompassing social world. For many enthusiasts this involvement is as exciting as the central activity itself and, in career volunteer work, often indistinguishable from it.

The routine of some serious leisure can constitute yet another appealing feature for those with severely shortened workweeks or no work at all. A wide variety of amateur activities require regular practice and rehearsal sessions, and volunteers are often asked to serve at their posts during certain hours on certain days of the week. People who miss the routine of the full-time job can find a fulfilling equivalent in a variety of serious leisure pursuits. Indeed, their job or former job may not foster self-development or self-fulfillment in nearly the same degree that their serious leisure does.

Substitute Lifestyle and Identity

We also saw earlier that serious leisure (and devotee work) offers a major lifestyle and identity for its participants, and I should now like to add that both can serve as solid substitutes for the ones they once knew in their work. Moreover, some lifestyles serve to identify their participants. In other words, the participants are members of a category of humankind who recognize themselves and, to some extent, are recognized by the larger community for the distinctive mode of life they lead. This is certainly true for the enthusiasts in some of the casual and many of the serious pursuits.

It was observed in chapter 2 that a profound lifestyle awaits anyone routinely pursuing a serious leisure career in, say, amateur theater, volunteer work with the mentally handicapped, the hobbyist card game of Trex (described in chapter 4), or the hobby of mountain climbing. And this person may also find exciting, albeit clearly less profound, a lifestyle in such casual leisure pastimes as socializing in the local hookah bar or in a nearby suq. But many other forms of casual leisure, for example, beachcombing or watching television are seldom shared with large numbers of other people; therefore they fail to qualify as group lifestyles as set out earlier. Moreover, in themselves, these activities are too superficial and unremarkable to serve as the basis for a recognizable mode of living where lifestyle is part of identity.

Substitute Central Life Interest

Finally, we have seen that, to the extent that lifestyles form around complicated, absorbing, satisfying activities, they can also be viewed as behavioral expressions of the participants' central life interests (Dubin 1992) in those activities. In the present-day Information Age, with its dwindling employment opportunities, most men and women everywhere on the planet will find more and more that the only kinds of central life interests open to them are the various amateur, hobbyist, and career volunteer activities composing serious leisure. Additionally, more and more of the underemployed will find themselves with a choice never before encountered in the history of work in the industrialized world: whether to make their, say, twenty-five-hour-a-week job their central life interest or turn to a serious leisure activity for this kind of attachment because the job is too insubstantial for an investment of positive emotional, physical, and intellectual energy. Of course, for the large majority of the unemployed and retired, serious leisure is their only recourse, if they are to have a central life interest at all. And there will always be a comparatively small number of people with sufficient time, energy, and opportunity to sustain more than one central life interest in either leisure or work and leisure.

As happens with leisure lifestyle, a leisure identity arises in conjunction with a leisure-based central life interest. In other words, the lifestyle of the participants in a given serious leisure activity expresses their central life interest there, while forming the basis for their personal and communal identity as people who go in for that activity. In the future, jobless or relatively jobless as it will be for many people, serious leisure will be the only remaining area in life where they can find an identity related to their distinctive personal qualities, qualities expressed in the course of realizing the rewards and benefits of serious leisure. Moreover, in the Information Age, such leisure will be the only remaining area where these people can find a community role capable of fostering significant self-respect. When seen in the light of the importance of work in many societies, most of the casual leisure activities with their strong appeal of immediate intrinsic reward (hedonism) are usually dismissed as adding little to their participants' self-respect. They offer no substitute for work.

The Probability

What are the chances that serious leisure, project-based leisure, and community involvement will become the substitute just considered? Put otherwise, how much must the MENA change to make this transformation a reality? From yet another angle, can the MENA change enough to permit this level of transformation?

Democracy—How Essential?

Must the governments of the countries in the MENA be substantially democratic for the possibility just sketched to be viable? If the answer to this question is affirmative, the possibility will be a long time in coming. So I stand by my skeptical outlook expressed at the end of chapter 5: obstacles like fissiparousness/oppositionalism, corporate weakness, and state dominance described near the end of chapter 1 suggest strongly that governmental democracy is a distant dream, in good part because these features of Arab/Iranian life will not pass soon. As an example, consider in 2012 the possibility of civil war erupting in Iraq, as sectarian autocracy threatens to undermine its fragile democracy (Allawi, Al-Nujaifi, and Al-Essawi 2011). At least a generation will have to move on, leaving the youth of today—the biggest boosters of democracy in the contemporary MENA—in ever greater control. Even then, what Levin (2007) says about democracy among American youth applies even more to their counterparts in the MENA. Too many of today's young Americans, he holds, lack the skills needed for citizen participation, a central process in any successful democracy. And this is occurring even though opportunities for such participation are increasing, as in the recent decision by King Abdullah of Saudi Arabia to grant women the right to vote and run for office in municipal elections (MacFarquhar 2011).

In short, we could end this book here were governmental democracy essential to pursuing serious and project-based leisure and community involvement. It would then be a book about a distant world, a futurology of the MENA, as it were. Nevertheless, there are rays of hope for cultural development in the present, which does depend in part on a kind of democracy, albeit one lying largely beyond the clutches of the politico-religious establishment.

Leisure Can Prevail

Let us start this section with Djaït's (2011, 166) observation that the lack of democracy in the MENA includes a refusal of fundamental liberties and rights. Though he fails to mention the right of leisure, this right *is* enshrined in the Constitution of the United Nations. According to its Clause 24, "everyone has the right to rest and leisure, including reasonable limitation of working hours and periodic holidays with pay." Is this right among those said to be missing in the MENA?

No, when considering leisure and devotee work, the future of the MENA looks noticeably brighter. For, whereas the Arabs and Iranians of the MENA lack the political experience that comes with citizen participation, an unknown, although I believe significant, proportion of them have some experience in collective activities in other kinds of work and leisure and in community involvement. We have seen in chapters 3 through 7 that this has been occurring in both the past and the present in certain arts, sports, hobbies, and volunteer roles. Participants gain this experience despite the three cultural obstacles so characteristic of the region.

Thus some people in the MENA, while engaging in work or leisure, are familiar with what it is like to associate with fellow citizens outside their tribal, ethnic or religious group. One consequence of such experience is that, as they participate in running grassroots groups, clubs, and associations that help make possible their collective activity, they learn how democracy works. True, this observation does rest on the assumption that these entities are democratically constituted, which in the West as nonprofits they necessarily are. In the West such groups, in being founded, operated, and dissolved, are legally required to adhere to a set of democratic procedures. But, since nonprofit groups are, by definition, established by their members for their members, it is likely that in the MENA, as well, such entities are most probably founded and run democratically, apart from any legal requirement to operate this way.

The nonprofit is one form of grassroots association (Smith 2000). Other less formal grassroots organizations also spring up around leisure activities, often taking the title of club or group. Here, too, some kind of democratic procedure tends to be the dominant form of governance, for members dissatisfied with how they are run would quit them were they to become disagreeably authoritarian. These entities are, after all, established for the pursuit of leisure, which is uncoerced. Dictatorial rule by one or a few members will soon force out other members who also want their say, but who also have other free-time alternatives to which they may turn. These essential workings of the grassroots leisure organizations bring us back to the earlier generalization that leisure interests are often capable of overriding social divisions.

At the face-to-face level in a leisure and devotee work activity, especially the serious pursuits and project-based varieties, it is, for example, more important to have an excellent striker in football (soccer), who happens to be Christian, than a mediocre one, who happens to be Muslim. With their outstanding striker, the mostly Muslim team has a manifestly improved chance of winning games, a cardinal reason for joining it. Outside the MENA, the Grootbos Foundation in South Africa has had success building sport facilities and organizing sports events designed to encourage participation among youth across the usual social barriers in the local community.[48]

To my knowledge, the Qur'an does not interdict such association with non-Muslims. But, if it did or if the state made it illegal to do so, then these politico-religious constraints in this area of leisure and devotee work would surely reduce participation for some members of the country and attenuate the experience of the activity for some others. This example demonstrates where the fault line can appear in the free pursuit of work and leisure activity in totalitarian and near totalitarian societies.

Be that as it may, our earlier chapters indicate that people in the MENA engage in a fair range of the leisure interests encompassed by the SLP. Many of these interests are pursued with at least one other person. Moreover, even work and leisure whose core activity is solitary may put the participant in contact with others by way of certain peripheral activities, such as participating in a group exhibition of a craft or attending a meeting of an organization that fosters a particular pursuit (e.g., an astronomical society, a surfers' club).

Such leisure is exemplified in the extreme by Tawakkol Karman, who won the Nobel Peace Prize in October 2011, one singular outcome of her community involvement. She is a human rights activist and mother of three children living in Yemen. Kasinof and Worth (2011) quote Nadia Mostafa, a professor of international relations at Cairo University: "Giving it [the Nobel Prize] to a woman and an Islamist? That means a sort of re-evaluation.... It means Islam is not against peace, it's not against women, and Islamists can be women activists, and they can fight for human rights, freedom, and democracy." Additionally, Walseth and Fasting (2003) found in a sample of Egyptian women who supported a fundamentalist interpretation of Islam that they believe the religion encourages their participation in sport. Pfister's (2010) research on female athletes from Islamic countries competing in the Olympic Games reveals that their participation in these events is shaped by a distinctive combination of opportunities and barriers found in the countries they represent. In brief, there is some evidence that leisure is prevailing in the MENA, with the suggestion that it will continue to do so. To be sure, such change depends on how the powers that be interpret the Qur'an and use their might to enforce that interpretation.

Gender

The example above featuring the striker in football is about a single-sex activity; everywhere in the world males and females usually play on sexually homogeneous sports teams. But in other spheres of work and leisure the two sexes frequently participate together. Theater, music, and dance number among the many kinds of mixed activity. We have seen earlier that (usually female) gender restrictions, whether governmental or religious, have been receding in these and other areas of free time. As for the restrictions that remain—and there still are many—they and their enforcement are sometimes ignored and at other times confronted. Here the mixing of the sexes continues. But it happens at times, too, that the penalties are too severe to ignore, in which case the mixing usually ceases.

Leisure, as we saw in chapter 6, is clearly one of the flash points in gender relations in the MENA. Such activity there is contextualized, in significant part, by what tradition prescribes and proscribes in gender relations. Nonetheless, women in the larger cities in countries like Iran, Egypt, Jordan, and Morocco are refusing to take no for an answer. They are insisting that their work and leisure interests also be recognized (e.g., in experimental theater, mixed dance troupes, book club discussion sessions, and elite and nonelite sport), sometimes at substantial personal danger. In fact, when we can begin scientific study of serious leisure and devotee work in the MENA, we will surely enrich our theoretic understanding of its rewards and costs, an understanding that presently rests almost exclusively on Western data.

Community Involvement

This genre of leisure and work is often collective; its altruism is often directed toward a human target of benefits. Even when the target is environmental or material, collective action is required to reach shared goals of, say, reducing pollution or building homes with Habitat for Humanity. Nonprofit groups established for primarily altruistic reasons are also democratic entities and the foregoing discussion applies to them as well. Ruth McCambridge (2004) explains how this works:

> Because the nonprofit activity people become involved in on a voluntary basis is often connected to something that matters to them at an

emotional level, it has the potential of acting as an excellent training ground for any number of disciplines important to civil society and active democracy. It can, for instance, help people to understand first-hand what steps they might take to change circumstances that trouble them. This will likely provide them with enhanced knowledge and analytical skills about legislative and political systems, social history, media portrayal of issues that they care about, and a host of other topics. (349)

Elsewhere, individuals participating in social movements, interpersonal relationships, and small informal groups find leisure where formal governance is either unnecessary or impossible. Here, however, tradition is the usual guide to thought and behavior, while government remains on the sidelines unable or unwilling to intervene. Here, in following the constraints of tradition but sometimes by ignoring them, these volunteers find attractive casual, serious, and project-based leisure.

Whither Cultural Development in the MENA?

Leisure, work, and community involvement seem destined to thrive in the MENA. From what has been said, it is evident that their thriving will not, even in the medium term, be ideal—the two will face major constraints. A major part of the problem is that leisure, said earlier to be society's freest institution, must in the Arab/Iranian context contend with two powerful institutions primarily anchored in closed systems of thought and behavior. In religion the closed system is spiritual canon, in politics it is governing doctrine as formulated by the ruling group (e.g., party, junta, dynastic bloc). New ideas endangering the ideological heart of these systems so cherished by the established order, ideas leading to possible social change, ideas born in the world of free time, will find it difficult, if not impossible, to penetrate and transform those systems.

But cultural development through the serious pursuits and project-based leisure will nevertheless continue. The absence of governmental democracy, though an impediment, will be insufficient to stifle the vast interest in leisure evident throughout the region. To the extent that the Arab Spring is centered on free-time activities, it is already succeeding, a process that had begun long ago.

The role of the West in helping to shape leisure in the MENA is difficult to describe with any precision. Earlier chapters have revealed an eagerness to adopt Western leisure, especially its popular

Katz, J. (1988). *Seductions of crime: Moral and sensual attractions of doing evil.* New York: Basic Books.

Kay, T. (1990). Active unemployment—A leisure pattern for the future. *Loisir et Société/Society and Leisure,* 12, 413–430.

Keyes, C.L.M. (1998). Social well-being. *Social Psychology Quarterly,* 61, 121–140.

Kuran, T. (2010). *The long divergence: How Islamic law held back the Middle East.* Princeton, NJ: Princeton University Press.

Laslett, P. (1994). The third age, the fourth age and the future. *Aging and Society,* 14, 436–447.

Layard, R. (2005). *Happiness: Lessons from a new science.* New York: Penguin.

Leadbeater, C., and Miller, P. (2004). *The pro-am revolution: How enthusiasts are changing our economy and society.* London, UK: Demos.

Levine, P. (2007). *The future of democracy: Developing the next generation of American citizens.* Medford, MA: Tufts University Press.

Lexová, I. (2000). *Ancient Egyptian dances,* trans. by K. Haltmar. Mineola, NY: Dover.

Lobo, F., and Watkins, G. (1995). Mature-aged unemployment and leisure. *World Leisure and Recreation,* 36 (4), 22–28.

Loughran, G. (1972). Games Arabs play. *Saudi Aramco World,* 23(summer), online edition (retrieved 5 July 2011).

Lunde, P. (1994). The Giralda. *Saudi Aramco World,* 45 (1, January–February), online edition (retrieved 2 July 2011).

Lyng, S. (1990). Edgework: A social psychological analysis of voluntary risk-taking. *American Journal of Sociology,* 95, 851–886.

Lyons, K., and Dionigi, R. (2007). Transcending emotional community: A qualitative examination of older adults and Masters' sports participation. *Leisure Sciences,* 29, 375–389.

MacFarquhar, N. (2011), Saudi monarch grants women right to vote. *New York Times,* 25 September, online edition.

Maffesoli, M. (1996). *The time of the tribes: The decline of individualism,* trans. by D. Smith. London, UK: Sage Publications.

Mannell, R.C. (1993). High investment activity and life satisfaction among older adults: Committed, serious leisure, and flow activities. In J.R. Kelly (Ed.), *Activity and aging: Staying involved in later life* (125–145). Newbury Park, CA: Sage.

Mannell, R.C., Kleiber, D.A., and Staempfli, M. (2006). Psychology and social psychology and the study of leisure. In C. Rojek, S.M. Shaw, and A.J. Veal (Eds.), *A handbook of leisure studies* (109–124). New York: Palgrave Macmillan.

Marcus, S.L. (2006). *Music in Egypt: Experiencing music, expressing culture.* New York: Oxford University Press.

McCambridge, R. (2004). Underestimating the power of nonprofit governance. *Nonprofit and Voluntary Sector Quarterly,* 33, 346–354.

Media Line Staff, the (2011). Saudi literary clubs told to do business by the book, 11 May. (Source: AHN [All Headline News, http://piratebricks.com/saudi-literary-clubs-told-to-do-business-by-the-book).

Menary, S. (2009). FIFA's Iraq ban has no impact. www.playthegame.org (retrieved 28 November 2011).

Miksell, M. (1958). The role of tribal markets in Morocco: Examples from the "Northern Zone." *Geographical Review*, 48, 494–511.

Myers, S.L., and Kirkpatrick, D.D. (2011). Egypt vows to end crackdown on non-profits. *New York Times*, Friday, 30 December (online edition).

Nahrstedt, W. (2000). Global edutainment: The role of leisure education for community development. In A. Sivan and H. Ruskin (Eds.), *Leisure education, community development and populations with special needs* (65–74). London: CAB International.

New York Times (2011). Yemen—protests (2011), updated 6 June (online edition).

NS Enterprizes (2008). Award Winning Documentary: Belly Dancers of Cairo. Source: http://www.natashasenkovich.com/cairo.php (retrieved 19 July 2011).

Nydell, M. (2006). *Understanding Arabs: A guide to modern times*, 4th ed. Boston, MA: Intercultural Press.

O'Brien, D. (2000). A falconer's memoire. Arlington, VA: PBS/SDPB, online edition (from http://www.pbs.org/falconer/index.htm, retrieved 7 July 2011).

O'Neill, J. (1973). Backgammon comes back . . . or was it ever away? *Saudi Aramco World*, 24(July/August), online edition (retrieved 7 July 2011).

Onyx, J., Leonard, R., and Hayward-Brown, H. (2003). The special position of volunteers in the formation of social capital. *Voluntary Action*, 6(1), 59–74.

Pearce, J.L. (1993). *Volunteers: The organizational behaviour of unpaid workers*, London, U.K.: Routledge.

Pfister, G. (2009). Islam and women's sports. Patheos.com, 16 October (http://www.patheos.com/Resources/Additional-Resources/Islam-and-Womens-Sports.html, (retrieved 26 October 2011).

Pfister, G. (2010). Outsiders: Muslim women and Olympic Games—barriers and opportunities. *International Journal of the History of Sport*, 27(16–18), 2925–2957.

Pinker, S. (2011). *The better angels of our nature: Why violence has declined*. New York: Viking.

Powell, D. (2003). Line dance Sydney. (source: http://www.roots-boots.net/ldance/history.html, retrieved 3 September 2011).

Price, M. (2011). Rituals of circumcision. Iran Chamber Society (source: http://www.iranchamber.com/culture/articles/rituals_of_circumcision.php, retrieved 18July 2011).

Putnam, R.D. (2000). *Bowling alone: The collapse and revival of American community*. New York: Simon and Schuster.

Racy, A.J. (1992). Arab music—Part one and Part two. In J. Hayes (Ed.), *The genius of Arab civilization: Source of renaissance*, 3rd ed. (chap. 1). New York: New York University Press.

Rapoport, R.N., and Rapoport, R. (1975). *Leisure and the family life cycle*. London, UK: Routledge and Kegan Paul.

Reid, D. (1995). *Work and leisure in the 21st century: From production to citizenship*. Toronto: Wall and Emerson.

Rogan, E. (2011). *The Arabs: A history*. New York: Basic Books.

Rojek, C. (2000). *Leisure and culture*. Houndmills, Basingstoke, UK: Palgrave Macmillan.

Rojek, C. (2002). Civil labour, leisure and post work society. *Société et Loisir/Society and Leisure*, 25, 21–36.

Rosen, N. (2011). How it started in Yemen: From Tahrir to Taghyir. *Jadaliyya*, 18 March (online edition).

Salzman, P.C. (2008). The Middle East's tribal DNA. *Middle East Quarterly*, 15(1), online edition.

Saudi Gazette (2010). Khoja-opens-Childrens-Day-festival-in-Riyadh, 30 November (30 November). (Source: http://www.a1saudiarabia.com/Khoja-opens-Childrens-Day-festival-in-Riyadh, retrieved 24 July 2011).

Shaikh H. (2007). "Act" formed to energise Riyadh's cultural scene. *Khaleej Times Online* 22 December (source: http://www.khaleejtimes.com/DisplayArticle-New.asp?xfile=data/middleeast/2007/December/middleeast_December326.xml&section=middleeast&col, retrieved 22 July 2011).

Shamir, B. (1985). Unemployment and "free time"—The role of the Protestant ethic and work involvement. *Leisure Studies*, 4, 333–345.

Siegenthaler, K.L., and O'Dell, I. (2003). Older golfers: Serious leisure and successful aging. *World Leisure Journal*, 45(1), 45–52.

Smith, D.H. (2000). *Grassroots associations*. Thousand Oaks, CA: Sage Publications.

Smith, D.H., Stebbins, R.A., and Dover, M. (2006). *A dictionary of nonprofit terms and concepts*. Bloomington, IN: Indiana University Press.

Sparre, K. (2006). FIFA punishes Iran's government for interfering in football. www.playthegame.org (retrieved 28 November 2011).

Spracklen, K. (2011). *Constructing leisure: Historical and philosophical debates*. Houndmills, Basingstoke, UK: Palgrave Macmillan.

Stebbins, R.A. (1976). Music among friends: The social networks of amateur musicians. *International Review of Sociology* (Series II), 12 (April–August), 52–73.

Stebbins, R.A. (1979). *Amateurs: On the margin between work and leisure*. Beverly Hills, CA: Sage (also available at www.seriousleisure.net— Digital Library).

Stebbins, R.A. (1981). The social psychology of selfishness. *Canadian Review of Sociology and Anthropology*, 18, 82–92.

Stebbins, R.A. (1982). Serious leisure: a conceptual statement. *Pacific Sociological Review*, 25, 251–272.

Stebbins, R.A. (1990). *The laugh-makers: Stand-up comedy as art, business, and life-style*. Montréal, QC and Kingston, ON: McGill-Queen's University Press.

Stebbins, R.A. (1992). *Amateurs, professionals, and serious leisure*. Montreal, QC and Kingston, ON: McGill-Queen's University Press.

Stebbins, R.A. (1993). *Career, culture and social psychology in a variety art: The magician* (reprinted ed.). Malabar, FL: Krieger.

Stebbins, R.A. (1994a). The liberal arts hobbies: A neglected subtype of serious leisure. *Loisir et Société/Society and Leisure*,16, 173–186.

Stebbins, R.A. (1994b). *The Franco-Calgarians: French language, leisure, and linguistic lifestyle in an anglophone city*. Toronto, ON: University of Toronto Press.

Stebbins, R.A. (1995). Leisure and selfishness: An exploration. In G. S. Fain (Ed.), *Reflections on the philosophy of leisure, Vol. II, Leisure and ethics* (292–303). Reston, VA: American Alliance for Health, Physical Education, Recreation, and Dance.

Stebbins, R.A. (1996a). *Tolerable differences: Living with deviance* (2nd ed). Toronto, ON: McGraw-Hill Ryerson (also available at www.seriousleisure.net—Digital Library).

Stebbins, R.A. (1996b). Volunteering: A serious leisure perspective. *Nonprofit and Voluntary Action Quarterly,* 25, 211–224.

Stebbins, R.A. (1996c). *The barbershop singer: Inside the social world of a musical hobby.* Toronto, ON: University of Toronto Press.

Stebbins, R.A. (1998). *After work: The search for an optimal leisure lifestyle.* Calgary, AB: Detselig. (now available at www.seriousleisure.net—Digital Library).

Stebbins, R.A. (2000a). Obligation as an aspect of leisure experience. *Journal of Leisure Research,* 32, 152–155.

Stebbins, R.A. (2000b). Optimal leisure lifestyle: Combining serious and casual leisure for personal well-being. In M.C. Cabeza (Ed.), *Leisure and human development: Proposals for the 6th World Leisure Congress* (101–107). Bilbao, Spain: University of Deusto.

Stebbins, R.A. (2001a). *New directions in the theory and research of serious leisure,* Mellen Studies in Sociology, vol. 28. Lewiston, NY: Edwin Mellen.

Stebbins, R.A. (2001b). Volunteering—mainstream and marginal: Preserving the leisure experience. In M. Graham and M. Foley (Eds.), *Volunteering in leisure: Marginal or inclusive?* (Vol. 75, 1–10). Eastbourne, UK: Leisure Studies Association.

Stebbins, R.A. (2001c). *Exploratory research in the social sciences.* Thousand Oaks, CA: Sage.

Stebbins, R.A. (2002). *The organizational basis of leisure participation: A motivational exploration.* State College, PA: Venture.

Stebbins, R.A. (2004a). *Between work and leisure: The common ground of two separate worlds.* New Brunswick, NJ: Transaction Publishers.

Stebbins, R.A. (2004b). Pleasurable aerobic activity: A type of casual leisure with salubrious implications. *World Leisure Journal,* 46(4), 55–58 (also available at www.seriousleisure.net—Digital Library, Other Works).

Stebbins, R.A. (2005a). *Challenging mountain nature: Risk, motive, and lifestyle in three hobbyist sports.* Calgary, AB: Detselig. (now available at www.seriousleisure.net—Digital Library).

Stebbins, R.A. (2005b). Project-based leisure: Theoretical neglect of a common use of free time. *Leisure Studies,* 24, 1–11.

Stebbins, R.A. (2006). Mentoring as a leisure activity: On the informal world of small-scale altruism. *World Leisure Journal,* 48(4), 3–10.

Stebbins, R.A. (2007a). *Serious leisure: A perspective for our time.* New Brunswick, NJ: Transaction.

Stebbins, R.A. (2007b). A leisure-based, theoretic typology of volunteers and volunteering. *Leisure Studies Association Newsletter,* 78 (November), 9–12 (also available at www.seriousleisure.net— Digital Library, "Leisure Reflections No.16").

Stebbins, R.A. (2009a). *Leisure and consumption: Common ground, separate worlds.* New York: Palgrave Macmillan.

Stebbins, R.A. (2009b). *Personal decisions in the public square: Beyond problem solving into a positive sociology.* New Brunswick, NJ: Transaction.

Stebbins, R.A. (2010a). Flow in serious leisure: Nature and prevalence. *Leisure Studies Association Newsletter,* 87 (November), 21–23 (also available at www.seriousleisure.net —Digital Library, "Leisure Reflections No. 25").

Stebbins, R.A. (2010b). Canada's world identity in sport: A legacy of winter. *Asian Journal of Canadian Studies,* 16(1–2), 1–30.

Stebbins, R.A. (2010c). Fulfilling leisure for youth. *YDI research brief number 6.* AgriLife Research and Extension, Texas A&M University (available at http://www.ydi.tamu.edu/briefs-and-reports).

Stebbins, R.A. (2011a). Leisure and happiness. *Leisure Studies Association Newsletter,* 90 (November), 18–20 (also available at www.seriousleisure.net—Digital Library, "Leisure Reflections No. 28").

Stebbins, R.A. (2011b). Personal memoirs, project-based leisure and therapeutic recreation for seniors. *Leisure Studies Association Newsletter,* 88 (March), 29–31 (also available at www.seriousleisure.net—Digital Library, "Leisure Reflections No. 26").

Stebbins, R.A. (2012). *The idea of leisure: First principles.* New Brunswick, NJ: Transaction.

Tisdall, S. (2011). Iran has been isolated by the Arab spring. *The Guardian,* Tuesday, 17 May (online edition at guardian.co.uk).

Touma, H.H. (2003). *The music of the Arabs,* trans. by L. Schwarts. Portland, OR: Amadeus.

Traditional Arab Music (2011). Arab music overview: Multi-Media Publishing: Crestline, CA (online edition http://www.traditionalarabicmusic.com/contact_us.htm, retrieved 18 July 2011).

Truzzi, M. (1972). The occult revival as popular culture. *The Sociological Quarterly,* 13, 16–36.

United Nations Development Program (2002). *Arab human development report: Creating opportunities for future generations.* New York: United Nations.

Unruh, D.R. (1979). Characteristics and types of participation in social worlds. *Symbolic Interaction,* 2, 115–130.

Unruh, D.R. (1980). The nature of social worlds. *Pacific Sociological Review,* 23, 271–296.

Upton, R. (2010). *Arab life: A history of a way of life.* Surrey, UK: Medina.

Usher, S. (2007). Arab youth revel in pop revolution. British Broadcasting Corporation, Monday, 21 May, online edition (retrieved 18 July 2011).

Walseth, K., and Fasting, K. (2003). Islam's view on physical activity and sport: Egyptian women interpreting Islam. *International Review of Sport Sociology,* 38(1), 45–60.

Weinblatt, N., and Navon, L. (1995). Flight from leisure: A neglected phenomenon in leisure studies. *Leisure Studies,* 17, 309–325.

Whitaker, B. (2000). The kidnappers' toll. www.al-bab.com (retrieved 24 November 2011).

World Casino Directory (2011). Source: http://www.worldcasinodirectory.com (retrieved 11 August 2011).

Worth, R.F. (2010). Yemen loses in soccer, but scores a p.r. victory. *New York Times,* Monday, 6 December (online edition).

Wuthnow, R. (1991). *Acts of compassion: Caring for others and helping ourselves.* Princeton, NJ: Princeton University Press.

Yoder, D.G. (1997). A model for commodity intensive serious leisure. *Journal of Leisure Research,* 29, 407–429.

Index